J. W. (John William) Mackail

The Holy Bible

Containing the Old and New Testaments: Vol. VI

J. W. (John William) Mackail

The Holy Bible
Containing the Old and New Testaments: Vol. VI

ISBN/EAN: 9783337100407

Printed in Europe, USA, Canada, Australia, Japan

Cover: Foto ©Lupo / pixelio.de

More available books at **www.hansebooks.com**

THE
HOLY BIBLE

CONTAINING THE

OLD AND NEW TESTAMENTS

TO WHICH IS PREFIXED AN INTRODUCTION

BY

J. W. MACKAIL

VOL. VI

EZEKIEL TO MALACHI

London
MACMILLAN AND CO., Limited
NEW YORK: THE MACMILLAN COMPANY
1898

GLASGOW: PRINTED AT THE UNIVERSITY PRESS
BY ROBERT MACLEHOSE AND CO.

THE BOOK OF THE PROPHET
EZEKIEL

NOW it came to pass in the thirtieth year, in the fourth month, in the fifth day of the month, as I was among the captives by the river of Chebar, that the heavens were opened, and I saw visions of God.

In the fifth day of the month, which was the fifth year of king Jehoiachin's captivity, the word of the Lord came expressly unto Ezekiel the priest, the son of Buzi, in the land of the Chaldeans by the river Chebar; and the hand of the Lord was there upon him.

And I looked, and, behold, a whirlwind came out of the north, a great cloud, and a fire infolding itself, and a brightness was about it, and out of the midst thereof as the colour of amber, out of the midst of the fire. Also out of the midst thereof came the likeness of four living creatures. And this was their appearance; they had the likeness of a man. And every one had four faces, and every one had four wings. And their feet were straight feet; and the sole of their feet was like the sole of a calf's foot: and they sparkled like the colour of burnished brass. And they had the hands of a man under their wings on their four sides; and they four had their faces and their wings. Their wings were joined one to another; they turned not when they went; they went every one straight forward. As for the likeness of their faces, they four had the face of a man, and the face of a lion, on the right side: and they four had the face of an ox on the left side; they four also had the face of an eagle. Thus were their faces: and their wings were stretched upward; two wings of every one were joined one to another, and two covered their bodies. And they went every one straight forward: whither the spirit was to go, they went; and they turned not when they went. As for the likeness of the living creatures, their appearance was like burning coals of fire, and like the appearance of lamps: it went up and down among the living creatures; and the fire was bright, and out of the fire went forth lightning. And the living creatures ran and returned as the appearance of a flash of lightning.

Now as I beheld the living creatures, behold one wheel upon the earth by the living creatures, with his four faces. The appearance of the wheels and their work was like unto the colour of a beryl: and they four had one likeness: and their appearance and their work was as it were a wheel in the middle of a wheel. When they went, they went upon their four sides: and they turned not when they went. As for their rings, they were so high that they were dreadful; and their rings were full of eyes round about them four. And when the living creatures went, the wheels went by them: and when the living creatures were lifted up from the earth, the wheels were lifted up. Whithersoever the spirit was to go, they went, thither was their spirit to go; and the wheels were lifted up over against them: for the spirit of the living creature was in the wheels. When those went, these went; and when those stood, these stood; and when those were lifted up from the earth, the wheels were lifted up over against them: for the spirit of the living creature was in the wheels. And the likeness of the firmament upon the heads of the living creature was as the colour of the terrible crystal, stretched forth over their heads above.

And under the firmament were their wings straight, the one toward the other: every one had two, which covered on this side, and every one had two, which covered on that side, their bodies. And when they went, I heard the noise of their wings, like the noise of great waters, as the voice of the Almighty, the voice of speech, as the noise of an host. When they stood, they let down their wings: and there was a voice from the firmament that was over their heads, when they stood, and had let down their wings.

And above the firmament that was over their

heads was the likeness of a throne, as the appearance of a sapphire stone: and upon the likeness of the throne was the likeness as the appearance of a man above upon it. And I saw as the colour of amber, as the appearance of fire round about within it, from the appearance of his loins even upward, and from the appearance of his loins even downward, I saw as it were the appearance of fire, and it had brightness round about. As the appearance of the bow that is in the cloud in the day of rain, so was the appearance of the brightness round about. This was the appearance of the likeness of the glory of the Lord.

And when I saw it, I fell upon my face, and I heard a voice of One that spake. And he said unto me, "Son of man, stand upon thy feet, and I will speak unto thee."

And the spirit entered into me when he spake unto me, and set me upon my feet, that I heard him that spake unto me. And he said unto me, "Son of man, I send thee to the children of Israel, to a rebellious nation that hath rebelled against me: they and their fathers have transgressed against me, even unto this very day: for they are impudent children and stiffhearted. I do send thee unto them; and thou shalt say unto them, Thus saith the Lord God. And they, whether they will hear, or whether they will forbear, (for they are a rebellious house,) yet shall know that there hath been a prophet among them. And thou, son of man, be not afraid of them, neither be afraid of their words, though briers and thorns be with thee, and thou dost dwell among scorpions: be not afraid of their words, nor be dismayed at their looks, though they be a rebellious house. And thou shalt speak my words unto them, whether they will hear, or whether they will forbear: for they are most rebellious. But thou, son of man, hear what I say unto thee; be not thou rebellious like that rebellious house: open thy mouth, and eat that I give thee."

And when I looked, behold, an hand was sent unto me; and, lo, a roll of a book was therein; and he spread it before me; and it was written within and without: and there was written therein lamentations, and mourning, and woe. Moreover he said unto me, "Son of man, eat that thou findest; eat this roll, and go speak unto the house of Israel." So I opened my mouth, and he caused me to eat that roll. And he said unto me, "Son of man, cause thy belly to eat, and fill thy bowels with this roll that I give thee." Then did I eat it; and it was in my mouth as honey for sweetness.

And he said unto me, "Son of man, go, get thee unto the house of Israel, and speak with my words unto them. For thou art not sent to a people of a strange speech and of an hard language, but to the house of Israel; not to many people of a strange speech and of an hard language, whose words thou canst not understand. Surely, had I sent thee to them, they would have hearkened unto thee: but the house of Israel will not hearken unto thee; for they will not hearken unto me: for all the house of Israel are impudent and hardhearted. Behold, I have made thy face strong against their faces, and thy forehead strong against their foreheads. As an adamant, harder than flint, have I made thy forehead: fear them not, neither be dismayed at their looks, though they be a rebellious house."

Moreover he said unto me, "Son of man, all my words that I shall speak unto thee receive in thine heart, and hear with thine ears. And go, get thee to them of the captivity, unto the children of thy people, and speak unto them, and tell them, Thus saith the Lord God; whether they will hear, or whether they will forbear."

Then the spirit took me up, and I heard behind me a voice of a great rushing, saying, "Blessed be the glory of the Lord from his place." I heard also the noise of the wings of the living creatures that touched one another, and the noise of the wheels over against them, and a noise of a great rushing. So the spirit lifted me up, and took me away, and I went in bitterness, in the heat of my spirit; but the hand of the Lord was strong upon me. Then I came to them of the captivity at Tel-abib, that dwelt by the river of Chebar, and I sat where they sat, and remained there astonished among them seven days.

And it came to pass at the end of seven days, that the word of the Lord came unto me, saying, "Son of man, I have made thee a watchman unto the house of Israel: therefore hear the word at my mouth, and give them warning from me.

"When I say unto the wicked, Thou shalt surely die; and thou givest him not warning, nor speakest to warn the wicked from his wicked way, to save his life; the same wicked man shall die in his iniquity; but his blood will I require at thine hand. Yet if thou warn the wicked, and he turn not from his wickedness, nor from his wicked way, he shall die in his iniquity; but thou hast delivered thy soul.

"Again, when a righteous man doth turn from his righteousness, and commit iniquity, and I lay a stumblingblock before him, he shall die: because thou hast not given him warning, he shall die in his sin, and his righteousness which he hath done shall not be remembered; but his blood will I require at thine hand. Nevertheless if thou warn the righteous man, that the righteous sin not, and he doth not sin, he shall surely live, because he is warned; also thou hast delivered thy soul."

And the hand of the Lord was there upon me; and he said unto me, "Arise, go forth into the plain, and I will there talk with thee." Then I arose, and went forth into the plain: and, behold, the glory of the Lord stood there, as the glory which I saw by the river of Chebar: and I fell on my face. Then the spirit entered into me, and set me upon my feet, and spake with me, and said unto me, "Go, shut thyself within thine house. But thou, O son of man, behold, they shall put bands upon thee, and shall bind thee with them, and thou shalt not go out among them: and I will make thy tongue cleave to the roof of thy mouth, that thou shalt be dumb, and shalt not be to them a reprover: for they are a rebellious house. But when I speak with thee, I will open thy mouth, and thou shalt say unto them, Thus saith the Lord God; He that heareth, let him hear; and he that forbeareth, let him forbear: for they are a rebellious house.

"Thou also, son of man, take thee a tile, and lay it before thee, and portray upon it the city, even Jerusalem: and lay siege against it, and build a fort against it, and cast a mount against it; set the camp also against it, and set battering rams against it round about. Moreover take thou unto thee an iron pan, and set it for a wall of iron between thee and the city: and set thy face against it, and it shall be besieged, and thou shalt lay siege against it. This shall be a sign to the house of Israel. Lie thou also upon thy left side, and lay the iniquity of the house of Israel upon it: according to the number of the days that thou shalt lie upon it thou shalt bear their iniquity. For I have laid upon thee the years of their iniquity, according to the number of the days, three hundred and ninety days: so shalt thou bear the iniquity of the house of Israel. And when thou hast accomplished them, lie again on thy right side, and thou shalt bear the iniquity of the house of Judah forty days: I have appointed thee each day for a year. Therefore thou shalt set thy face toward the siege of Jerusalem, and thine arm shall be uncovered, and thou shalt prophesy against it. And, behold, I will lay bands upon thee, and thou shalt not turn thee from one side to another, till thou hast ended the days of thy siege.

"Take thou also unto thee wheat, and barley, and beans, and lentiles, and millet, and vetches, and put them in one vessel, and make thee bread thereof; according to the number of the days that thou shalt lie upon thy side, three hundred and ninety days shalt thou eat thereof. And thy meat which thou shalt eat shall be by weight, twenty shekels a day: from time to time shalt thou eat it. Thou shalt drink also water by measure, the sixth part of an hin: from time to time shalt thou drink. And thou shalt eat it as barley cakes, and thou shalt bake it with dung that cometh out of man, in their sight."

And the Lord said, "Even thus shall the children of Israel eat their defiled bread among the Gentiles, whither I will drive them." Then said I, "Ah Lord God! behold, my soul hath not been polluted: for from my youth up even till now have I not eaten of that which dieth of itself, or is torn in pieces; neither came there abominable flesh into my mouth." Then he said unto me, "Lo, I have given thee cow's dung for man's dung, and thou shalt prepare thy bread therewith." Moreover he said unto me, "Son of man, behold, I will break the staff of bread in Jerusalem: and they shall eat bread by weight, and with care; and they shall drink water by measure, and with astonishment: that they may want bread and water, and be astonied one with another, and consume away for their iniquity.

"And thou, son of man, take thee a sharp knife, take thee a barber's razor, and cause it to pass upon thine head and upon thy beard: then take the balances to weigh, and divide the hair. Thou shalt burn with fire a third part in the midst of the city, when the days of the siege are fulfilled: and thou shalt take a third part, and smite about it with a knife: and a third part thou shalt scatter in the wind; and I will draw out a sword after them. Thou shalt also take thereof a few in number, and bind them in thy skirts. Then take of them again, and cast them into the midst of the fire, and burn them in the fire; for thereof shall a fire come forth into all the house of Israel.

"Thus saith the Lord God; This is Jerusalem: I have set it in the midst of the nations and countries that are round about her. And she hath changed my judgments into wickedness more than the nations, and my statutes more than the countries that are round about her: for they have refused my judgments and my statutes, they have not walked in them. Therefore thus saith the Lord God; Because ye multiplied more than the nations that are round about you, and have not walked in my statutes, neither have kept my judgments, neither have done according to the judgments of the nations that are round about you; therefore thus saith the Lord God; Behold, I, even I, am against thee, and will execute judgments in the midst of thee in the sight of the nations. And I will do in thee that which I have not done, and whereunto I will not do any more the like, because of all thine abominations. Therefore the fathers shall eat the sons in the midst of thee, and the sons shall eat their fathers; and I will execute judgments in thee, and the whole remnant of thee will I scatter into all the winds.

"Wherefore, as I live, saith the Lord God, surely, because thou hast defiled my sanctuary with all thy detestable things, and with all thine abominations, therefore will I also diminish thee; neither shall mine eye spare, neither will I have any pity. A third part of thee shall die with the pestilence, and with famine shall they be consumed in the midst of thee: and a third part shall fall by the sword round about thee; and I will scatter a third part into all the winds, and I will draw out a sword after them. Thus shall mine anger be accomplished, and I will cause my fury to rest upon them, and I will be comforted: and they shall know that I the Lord have spoken it in my zeal, when I have accomplished my fury in them.

"Moreover I will make thee waste, and a reproach among the nations that are round about thee, in the sight of all that pass by. So it shall be a reproach and a taunt, an instruction and an astonishment unto the nations that are round about thee, when I shall execute judgments in thee in anger and in fury and in furious rebukes; (I the Lord have spoken it;) when I shall send upon them the evil arrows of famine, which shall be for their destruction, and which I will send to destroy you: and I will increase the famine upon you, and will break your staff of bread: so will I send upon you famine and evil beasts, and they shall bereave thee; and pestilence and blood shall pass through thee; and I will bring the sword upon thee. I the Lord have spoken it."

And the word of the Lord came unto me, saying,

"Son of man, set thy face toward the mountains of Israel, and prophesy against them, and say, Ye mountains of Israel, hear the word of the Lord God; Thus saith the Lord God to the mountains, and to the hills, to the rivers, and to the valleys; Behold, I, even I, will bring a sword upon you, and I will destroy your high places. And your altars shall be desolate, and your images shall be broken: and I will cast down your slain men before your idols. And I will lay the dead carcases of the children of Israel before their idols; and I will scatter your bones round about your altars. In all your dwellingplaces the cities shall be laid waste, and the high places shall be desolate; that your altars may be laid waste and made desolate, and your idols may be broken and cease, and your images may be cut down, and your works may be abolished. And the slain shall fall in the midst of you, and ye shall know that I am the Lord.

"Yet will I leave a remnant, that ye may

have some that shall escape the sword among the nations, when ye shall be scattered through the countries. And they that escape of you shall remember me among the nations whither they shall be carried captives, because I am broken with their whorish heart, which hath departed from me, and with their eyes, which go a whoring after their idols: and they shall loathe themselves for the evils which they have committed in all their abominations. And they shall know that I am the Lord, and that I have not said in vain that I would do this evil unto them.

"Thus saith the Lord God; Smite with thine hand, and stamp with thy foot, and say, Alas for all the evil abominations of the house of Israel! for they shall fall by the sword, by the famine, and by the pestilence. He that is far off shall die of the pestilence; and he that is near shall fall by the sword; and he that remaineth and is besieged shall die by the famine: thus will I accomplish my fury upon them. Then shall ye know that I am the Lord, when their slain men shall be among their idols round about their altars, upon every high hill, in all the tops of the mountains, and under every green tree, and under every thick oak, the place where they did offer sweet savour to all their idols. So will I stretch out my hand upon them, and make the land desolate, yea, more desolate than the wilderness toward Diblath, in all their habitations: and they shall know that I am the Lord."

Moreover the word of the Lord came unto me, saying,

"Also, thou son of man, thus saith the Lord God unto the land of Israel; An end, the end is come upon the four corners of the land. Now is the end come upon thee, and I will send mine anger upon thee, and will judge thee according to thy ways, and will recompense upon thee all thine abominations. And mine eye shall not spare thee, neither will I have pity: but I will recompense thy ways upon thee, and thine abominations shall be in the midst of thee: and ye shall know that I am the Lord.

"Thus saith the Lord God; An evil, an only evil, behold, is come. An end is come, the end is come: it watcheth for thee; behold, it is come. The morning is come unto thee, O thou that dwellest in the land: the time is come, the day of trouble is near, and not the sounding again of the mountains. Now will I shortly pour out my fury upon thee, and accomplish mine anger upon thee: and I will judge thee according to thy ways, and will recompense thee for all thine abominations. And mine eye shall not spare, neither will I have pity: I will recompense thee according to thy ways and thine abominations that are in the midst of thee; and ye shall know that I am the Lord that smiteth.

"Behold the day, behold, it is come: the morning is gone forth; the rod hath blossomed: pride hath budded, violence is risen up into a rod of wickedness: none of them shall remain, nor of their multitude, nor of any of theirs, neither shall there be wailing for them.

"The time is come, the day draweth near: let not the buyer rejoice, nor the seller mourn: for wrath is upon all the multitude thereof. For the seller shall not return to that which is sold, although they were yet alive: for the vision is touching the whole multitude thereof, which shall not return; neither shall any strengthen himself in the iniquity of his life. They have blown the trumpet, even to make all ready; but none goeth to the battle: for my wrath is upon all the multitude thereof. The sword is without, and the pestilence and the famine within: he that is in the field shall die with the sword; and he that is in the city, famine and pestilence shall devour him. But they that escape of them shall escape, and shall be on the mountains like doves of the valleys, all of them mourning, every one for his iniquity.

"All hands shall be feeble, and all knees shall be weak as water. They shall also gird themselves with sackcloth, and horror shall cover them; and shame shall be upon all faces, and baldness upon all their heads. They shall cast their silver in the streets, and their gold shall be removed: their silver and their gold shall not be able to deliver them in the day of the wrath of the Lord: they shall not satisfy their souls, neither fill their bowels: because it is the stumblingblock of their iniquity.

"As for the beauty of his ornament, he set it in majesty: but they made the images of their abominations and of their detestable things therein: therefore have I set it far from them. And I will give it into the hands of the strangers for a prey, and to the wicked of the earth for a spoil; and they shall pollute it. My face will I turn also from them, and they shall pollute my secret place: for the robbers shall enter into it, and defile it.

"Make a chain: for the land is full of bloody crimes, and the city is full of violence. Wherefore I will bring the worst of the heathen, and they shall possess their houses: I will also make the pomp of the strong to cease; and their holy places shall be defiled. Destruction cometh; and they shall seek peace, and there shall be none. Mischief shall come upon mischief, and rumour shall be upon rumour; then shall they seek a vision of the prophet; but the law shall perish from the priest, and counsel from the ancients. The king shall mourn, and the prince shall be clothed with desolation, and the hands of the people of the land shall be troubled: I will do unto them after their way, and according to their deserts will I judge them; and they shall know that I am the Lord."

And it came to pass in the sixth year, in the sixth month, in the fifth day of the month, as I sat in mine house, and the elders of Judah sat before me, that the hand of the Lord God fell there upon me. Then I beheld, and lo a likeness as the appearance of fire: from the appearance of his loins even downward, fire; and from his loins even upward, as the appearance of brightness, as the colour of amber. And he put forth the form of an hand, and took me by a lock of mine head; and the Spirit lifted me up between the earth and the heaven, and brought me in the visions of God to Jerusalem, to the door of the inner gate that looketh toward the north; where was the seat of the image of jealousy, which provoketh to jealousy. And, behold, the glory of the God of Israel was there, according to the vision that I saw in the plain.

Then said he unto me, "Son of man, lift up thine eyes now the way toward the north." So I lifted up mine eyes the way toward the north, and behold northward at the gate of the altar this image of jealousy in the entry. He said furthermore unto me, "Son of man, seest thou what they do? even the great abominations that the house of Israel committeth here, that I should go far off from my sanctuary? but turn thee yet again, and thou shalt see greater abominations."

And he brought me to the door of the court; and when I looked, behold a hole in the wall. Then said he unto me, "Son of man, dig now in the wall." And when I had digged in the wall, behold a door: and he said unto me, "Go in, and behold the wicked abominations that they do here." So I went in and saw; and behold every form of creeping things, and abominable beasts, and all the idols of the house of Israel, portrayed upon the wall round about. And there stood before them seventy men of the ancients of the house of Israel, and in the midst of them stood Jaazaniah the son of Shaphan, with every man his censer in his hand; and a thick cloud of incense went up. Then said he unto me, "Son of man, hast thou seen what the ancients of the house of Israel do in the dark, every man in the chambers of his imagery? for they say, The Lord seeth us not; the Lord hath forsaken the earth."

He said also unto me, "Turn thee yet again, and thou shalt see greater abominations that they do." Then he brought me to the door of the gate of the Lord's house which was toward the north; and, behold, there sat women weeping for Tammuz.

Then said he unto me, "Hast thou seen this, O son of man? turn thee yet again, and thou shalt see greater abominations than these." And he brought me into the inner court of the Lord's house, and, behold, at the door of the temple of the Lord, between the porch and the altar, were about five and twenty men, with their backs toward the temple of the Lord, and their faces toward the east; and they worshipped the sun toward the east.

Then he said unto me, "Hast thou seen this, O son of man? Is it a light thing to the house of Judah that they commit the abominations which they commit here? for they have filled the land with violence, and have returned to provoke me to anger: and, lo, they put the branch to their nose. Therefore will I also deal in fury: mine eye shall not spare, neither will I have pity: and though they cry in mine ears with a loud voice, yet will I not hear them."

He cried also in mine ears with a loud voice, saying, "Cause them that have charge over the city to draw near, even every man with his destroying weapon in his hand." And, behold, six men came from the way of the higher gate, which lieth toward the north, and every man a slaughter weapon in his hand; and one man among them was clothed with linen, with a writer's inkhorn by his side: and they went in, and stood beside the brazen altar.

And the glory of the God of Israel was gone up from the cherub, whereupon he was, to the threshold of the house. And he called to the man clothed with linen, which had the writer's inkhorn by his side; and the Lord said unto him, "Go through the midst of the city, through the midst of Jerusalem, and set a mark upon the foreheads of the men that sigh and that cry for all the abominations that be done in the midst thereof." And to the others he said in mine hearing, "Go ye after him through the city, and smite: let not your eye spare, neither have ye pity: slay utterly old and young, both maids, and little children, and women: but come not near any man upon whom is the mark; and begin at my sanctuary." Then they began at the ancient men which were before the house. And he said unto them, "Defile the house, and fill the courts with the slain: go ye forth." And they went forth, and slew in the city.

And it came to pass, while they were slaying them, and I was left, that I fell upon my face, and cried, and said, "Ah Lord God! wilt thou destroy all the residue of Israel in thy pouring out of thy fury upon Jerusalem?" Then said he unto me, "The iniquity of the house of Israel and Judah is exceeding great, and the land is full of blood, and the city full of perverseness: for they say, The Lord hath forsaken the earth, and the Lord seeth not. And as for me also, mine eye shall not spare, neither will I have pity, but I will recompense their way upon their head."

And, behold, the man clothed with linen, which had the inkhorn by his side, reported the matter, saying, "I have done as thou hast commanded me." Then I looked, and, behold, in the firmament that was above the head of the cherubims there appeared over them as it were a sapphire stone, as the appearance of the likeness of a throne. And he spake unto the man clothed with linen, and said, "Go in between the wheels, even under the cherub, and fill thine hand with coals of fire from between the cherubims, and scatter them over the city." And he went in in my sight.

Now the cherubims stood on the right side of the house, when the man went in; and the cloud filled the inner court. Then the glory of the Lord went up from the cherub, and stood over the threshold of the house; and the house was filled with the cloud, and the court was full of the brightness of the Lord's glory. And the sound of the cherubims' wings was heard even to the outer court, as the voice of the Almighty God when he speaketh. And it came to pass, that when he had commanded the man clothed with linen, saying, "Take fire from between the wheels, from between the cherubims;" then he went in, and stood beside the wheels. And one cherub stretched forth his hand from between the cherubims unto the fire that was between the cherubims, and took thereof, and put it into the hands of him that was clothed with linen: who took it, and went out.

And there appeared in the cherubims the form of a man's hand under their wings. And when I looked, behold the four wheels by the cherubims, one wheel by one cherub, and another wheel by another cherub: and the appearance of the wheels was as the colour of a beryl stone. And as for their appearances, they four had one likeness, as if a wheel had been in the midst of a wheel. When they went, they went upon their four sides; they turned not as they went, but to the place whither the head looked they followed it; they turned not as they went. And their whole body, and their backs, and their hands, and their wings, and the wheels, were full of eyes round about, even the wheels that they four had.

As for the wheels, it was cried unto them in my hearing, "O wheel!" And every one had four faces: the first face was the face of a cherub, and the second face was the face of a man, and the third the face of a lion, and the fourth the face of an eagle. And the cherubims were lifted up. This is the living creature that I saw by the river of Chebar.

And when the cherubims went, the wheels

went by them: and when the cherubims lifted up their wings to mount up from the earth, the same wheels also turned not from beside them. When they stood, these stood; and when they were lifted up, these lifted up themselves also: for the spirit of the living creature was in them. Then the glory of the Lord departed from off the threshold of the house, and stood over the cherubims. And the cherubims lifted up their wings, and mounted up from the earth in my sight: when they went out, the wheels also were beside them, and every one stood at the door of the east gate of the Lord's house; and the glory of the God of Israel was over them above.

This is the living creature that I saw under the God of Israel by the river of Chebar; and I knew that they were the cherubims. Every one had four faces apiece, and every one four wings; and the likeness of the hands of a man was under their wings. And the likeness of their faces was the same faces which I saw by the river of Chebar, their appearances and themselves: they went every one straight forward.

Moreover the Spirit lifted me up, and brought me unto the east gate of the Lord's house, which looketh eastward: and behold at the door of the gate five and twenty men; among whom I saw Jaazaniah the son of Azur, and Pelatiah the son of Benaiah, princes of the people. Then said he unto me, "Son of man, these are the men that devise mischief, and give wicked counsel in this city; which say, It is not near; let us build houses: this city is the caldron, and we be the flesh. Therefore prophesy against them, prophesy, O son of man."

And the Spirit of the Lord fell upon me, and said unto me, "Speak; Thus saith the Lord; Thus have ye said, O house of Israel: for I know the things that come into your mind, every one of them. Ye have multiplied your slain in this city, and ye have filled the streets thereof with the slain. Therefore thus saith the Lord God; Your slain whom ye have laid in the midst of it, they are the flesh, and this city is the caldron: but I will bring you forth out of the midst of it. Ye have feared the sword; and I will bring a sword upon you, saith the Lord God. And I will bring you out of the midst thereof, and deliver you into the hands of strangers, and will execute judgments among you. Ye shall fall by the sword; I will judge you in the border of Israel; and ye shall know that I am the Lord. This city shall not be your caldron, neither shall ye be the flesh in the midst thereof; but I will judge you in the border of Israel: and ye shall know that I am the Lord: for ye have not walked in my statutes, neither executed my judgments, but have done after the manners of the heathen that are round about you."

And it came to pass, when I prophesied, that Pelatiah the son of Benaiah died. Then fell I down upon my face, and cried with a loud voice, and said, "Ah Lord God! wilt thou make a full end of the remnant of Israel?"

Again the word of the Lord came unto me, saying, "Son of man, thy brethren, even thy brethren, the men of thy kindred, and all the house of Israel wholly, are they unto whom the inhabitants of Jerusalem have said, Get you far from the Lord: unto us is this land given in possession. Therefore say, Thus saith the Lord God; Although I have cast them far off among the heathen, and although I have scattered them among the countries, yet will I be to them as a little sanctuary in the countries where they shall come. Therefore say, Thus saith the Lord God; I will even gather you from the people, and assemble you out of the countries where ye have been scattered, and I will give you the land of Israel. And they shall come thither, and they shall take away all the detestable things thereof and all the abominations thereof from thence. And I will give them one heart, and I will put a new spirit within you; and I will take the stony heart out of their flesh, and will give them an heart of flesh: that they may walk in my statutes, and keep mine ordinances, and do them: and they shall be my people, and I will be their God. But as for them whose heart walketh after the heart of their detestable things and their abominations, I will recompense their way upon their own heads, saith the Lord God."

Then did the cherubims lift up their wings, and the wheels beside them; and the glory of the God of Israel was over them above. And the glory of the Lord went up from the midst of the city, and stood upon the mountain which is on the east side of the city.

Afterwards the Spirit took me up, and brought me in a vision by the Spirit of God into Chaldea, to them of the captivity. So the vision that I had seen went up from me. Then I spake unto them of the captivity all the things that the Lord had shewed me.

The word of the Lord also came unto me, saying, "Son of man, thou dwellest in the midst of a rebellious house, which have eyes to see, and see not; they have ears to hear, and hear not: for they are a rebellious house. Therefore, thou son of man, prepare thee stuff for removing, and remove by day in their sight; and thou shalt remove from thy place to another place in their sight: it may be they will consider, though they be a rebellious house. Then shalt thou bring forth thy stuff by day in their sight, as stuff for removing: and thou shalt go forth at even in their sight, as they that go forth into captivity. Dig thou through the wall in their sight, and carry out thereby. In their sight shalt thou bear it upon thy shoulders, and carry it forth in the twilight: thou shalt cover thy face, that thou see not the ground: for I have set thee for a sign unto the house of Israel."

And I did so as I was commanded: I brought forth my stuff by day, as stuff for captivity, and in the even I digged through the wall with mine hand; I brought it forth in the twilight, and I bare it upon my shoulder in their sight.

And in the morning came the word of the Lord unto me, saying, "Son of man, hath not the house of Israel, the rebellious house, said unto thee, What doest thou? Say thou unto them, Thus saith the Lord God; This burden concerneth the prince in Jerusalem, and all the house of Israel that are among them. Say, I am your sign: like as I have done, so shall it be done unto them: they shall remove and go into captivity. And the prince that is among them shall bear upon his shoulder in the twilight, and shall go forth: they shall dig through the wall to carry out thereby: he shall cover his face, that he see not the ground with his eyes. My net also will I spread upon him, and he shall be taken in my snare: and I will bring him to Babylon to the land of the Chaldeans; yet shall he not see it, though he shall die there. And I will scatter toward every wind all that are about him to help him, and all his bands; and I will draw out the sword after them. And they shall know that I am the Lord, when I shall scatter them among the nations, and disperse them in the countries. But I will leave a few men of them from the sword, from the famine, and from the pestilence; that they may declare all their abominations among the heathen whither they come; and they shall know that I am the Lord."

Moreover the word of the Lord came to me, saying, "Son of man, eat thy bread with quaking, and drink thy water with trembling and with carefulness; and say unto the people of the land, Thus saith the Lord God of the inhabitants of Jerusalem, and of the land of Israel; They shall eat their bread with carefulness, and drink their water with astonishment, that her land may be desolate from all that is therein, because of the violence of all them that dwell therein. And the cities that are inhabited shall be laid waste, and the land shall be desolate; and ye shall know that I am the Lord."

And the word of the Lord came unto me, saying, "Son of man, what is that proverb that ye have in the land of Israel, saying, The days are prolonged, and every vision faileth? Tell them therefore, Thus saith the Lord God; I will make this proverb to cease, and they shall no more use it as a proverb in Israel; but say unto them, The days are at hand, and the effect of every vision. For there shall be no more any vain vision nor flattering divination within the house of Israel. For I am the Lord: I will speak, and the word that I shall speak shall come to pass; it shall be no more prolonged: for in your days, O rebellious house, will I say the word, and will perform it, saith the Lord God."

Again the word of the Lord came to me, saying, "Son of man, behold, they of the house of Israel say, The vision that he seeth is for many days to come, and he prophesieth of the times that are far off. Therefore say unto them, Thus saith the Lord God; There shall none of my words be prolonged any more, but the word which I have spoken shall be done, saith the Lord God."

And the word of the Lord came unto me, saying, "Son of man, prophesy against the prophets of Israel that prophesy, and say thou unto them that prophesy out of their own hearts, Hear ye the word of the Lord; thus saith the Lord God; Woe unto the foolish prophets, that follow their own spirit, and have seen nothing! O Israel, thy prophets are like the foxes in the deserts. Ye have not gone up into the gaps, neither made up the hedge for the house of Israel to stand in the battle in the day of the Lord. They have seen vanity and lying divination, saying, The Lord saith: and the Lord hath not sent them: and they have made others to hope that they would confirm the word. Have ye not seen a vain vision, and have ye not spoken a lying divination, whereas ye say, The Lord saith it; albeit I have not spoken?

"Therefore thus saith the Lord God; Because ye have spoken vanity, and seen lies, therefore, behold, I am against you, saith the Lord God. And mine hand shall be upon the prophets that see vanity, and that divine lies: they shall not be in the assembly of my people, neither shall they be written in the writing of the house of Israel, neither shall they enter into the land of Israel; and ye shall know that I am the Lord God. Because, even because they have seduced my people, saying, Peace; and there was no peace; and one built up a wall, and, lo, others daubed it with untempered mortar: say unto them which daub it with untempered mortar, that it shall fall: there shall be an overflowing shower; and ye, O great hailstones, shall fall; and a stormy wind shall rend it. Lo, when the wall is fallen, shall it not be said unto you, Where is the daubing wherewith ye have daubed it? Therefore thus saith the Lord God; I will even rend it with a stormy wind in my fury; and there shall be an overflowing shower in mine anger, and great hailstones in my fury to consume it. So will I break down the wall that ye have daubed with untempered mortar, and bring it down to the ground, so that the foundation thereof shall be discovered, and it shall fall, and ye shall be consumed in the midst thereof: and ye shall know that I am the Lord. Thus will I accomplish my wrath upon the wall, and upon them that have daubed it with untempered mortar, and will say unto you, The wall is no more, neither they that daubed it; to wit, the prophets of Israel which prophesy concerning Jerusalem, and which see visions of peace for her, and there is no peace, saith the Lord God.

"Likewise, thou son of man, set thy face against the daughters of thy people, which prophesy out of their own heart; and prophesy thou against them, and say, Thus saith the Lord God; Woe to the women that sew pillows to all armholes, and make kerchiefs upon the head of every stature to hunt souls! Will ye hunt the souls of my people, and will ye save the souls alive that come unto you? And will ye pollute me among my people for handfuls of barley and for pieces of bread, to slay the souls that should not die, and to save the souls alive that should not live, by your lying to my people that hear your lies? Wherefore thus saith the Lord God; Behold, I am against your pillows, wherewith ye there hunt the souls to make them fly, and I will tear them from your arms, and will let the souls go, even the souls that ye hunt to make them fly. Your kerchiefs also will I tear, and deliver my people out of your hand, and they shall be no more in your hand to be hunted; and ye shall know that I am the Lord.

"Because with lies ye have made the heart of the righteous sad, whom I have not made sad; and strengthened the hands of the wicked, that he should not return from his wicked way, by promising him life: therefore ye shall see no more vanity, nor divine divinations: for I will deliver my people out of your hand: and ye shall know that I am the Lord."

Then came certain of the elders of Israel unto me, and sat before me. And the word of the Lord came unto me, saying,

"Son of man, these men have set up their idols in their heart, and put the stumblingblock of their iniquity before their face: should I be enquired of at all by them? Therefore speak unto them, and say unto them, Thus saith the Lord God; Every man of the house of Israel that setteth up his idols in his heart, and putteth the stumblingblock of his iniquity before his face, and cometh to the prophet; I the Lord will answer him that cometh according to the multitude of his idols; that I may take the house of Israel in their own heart, because they are all estranged from me through their idols.

"Therefore say unto the house of Israel, Thus saith the Lord God; Repent, and turn yourselves from your idols; and turn away your faces from all your abominations. For every one of the house of Israel, or of the stranger that sojourneth in Israel, which separateth himself from me, and setteth up his idols in his heart, and putteth the stumblingblock of his iniquity before his face, and cometh to a prophet to enquire of him concerning me; I the Lord will answer him by myself: and I will set my face against that man, and will make him a sign and a proverb, and I will cut him off from the midst of my people; and ye shall know that I am the Lord. And if the prophet be deceived when he hath spoken a thing, I the Lord have deceived that prophet, and I will stretch out my hand upon him, and will destroy him from the midst of my people Israel. And they shall bear the punishment of their iniquity: the punishment of the prophet shall be even as the punishment of him that seeketh unto him; that the house of Israel may go no more astray from me, neither be polluted any more with all their transgressions; but that they may be my people, and I may be their God, saith the Lord God."

The word of the Lord came again to me, saying,

"Son of man, when the land sinneth against me by trespassing grievously, then will I stretch out mine hand upon it, and will break the staff of the bread thereof, and will send famine upon it, and will cut off man and beast from it: though these three men, Noah, Daniel, and Job, were in it, they should deliver but their own souls by their righteousness, saith the Lord God.

"If I cause noisome beasts to pass through the land, and they spoil it, so that it be desolate, that no man may pass through because of the beasts: though these three men were in it, as I live, saith the Lord God, they shall deliver neither sons nor daughters; they only shall be delivered, but the land shall be desolate.

"Or if I bring a sword upon that land, and say, Sword, go through the land; so that I cut off man and beast from it: though these three men were in it, as I live, saith the Lord God, they shall deliver neither sons nor daughters, but they only shall be delivered themselves.

"Or if I send a pestilence into that land, and pour out my fury upon it in blood, to cut off from it man and beast: though Noah, Daniel, and Job, were in it, as I live, saith the Lord God, they shall deliver neither son nor daughter; they shall but deliver their own souls by their righteousness.

"For thus saith the Lord God; How much more when I send my four sore judgments upon Jerusalem, the sword, and the famine, and the noisome beast, and the pestilence, to cut off from it man and beast? Yet, behold, therein shall be left a remnant that shall be brought forth, both sons and daughters: behold, they shall come forth unto you, and ye shall see their way and their doings: and ye shall be comforted concerning the evil that I have brought upon Jerusalem, even concerning all that I have brought upon it. And they shall comfort you, when ye see their ways and their doings: and ye shall know that I have not done without cause all that I have done in it, saith the Lord God."

And the word of the Lord came unto me, saying,

"Son of man, what is the vine tree more than any tree, or than a branch which is among the trees of the forest? Shall wood be taken thereof to do any work? or will men take a pin of it to hang any vessel thereon? Behold, it is cast into the fire for fuel; the fire devoureth both the ends of it, and the midst of it is burned. Is it meet for any work? Behold, when it was whole, it was meet for no work: how much less shall it be meet yet for any work, when the fire hath devoured it, and it is burned? Therefore thus saith the Lord God; As the vine tree among the trees of the forest, which I have given to the fire for fuel, so will I give the inhabitants of Jerusalem. And I will set my face against them; they shall go out from one fire, and another fire shall devour them; and ye shall know that I am the Lord, when I set my face against them. And I will make the land desolate, because they have committed a trespass, saith the Lord God."

Again the word of the Lord came unto me, saying,

"Son of man, cause Jerusalem to know her abominations, and say, Thus saith the Lord God unto Jerusalem; Thy birth and thy nativity is of the land of Canaan; thy father was an Amorite, and thy mother an Hittite. And as for thy nativity, in the day thou wast born thy navel was not cut, neither wast thou washed in water to supple thee; thou wast not salted at all, nor swaddled at all. None eye pitied thee, to do any of these unto thee, to have compassion upon thee; but thou wast cast out in the open field, to the loathing of thy person, in the day that thou wast born.

"And when I passed by thee, and saw thee polluted in thine own blood, I said unto thee when thou wast in thy blood, Live; yea, I said unto thee when thou wast in thy blood, Live. I have caused thee to multiply as the bud of the field, and thou hast increased and waxen great, and thou art come to excellent ornaments: thy breasts are fashioned, and thine hair is grown, whereas thou wast naked and bare.

Now when I passed by thee, and looked upon thee, behold, thy time was the time of love; and I spread my skirt over thee, and covered thy nakedness: yea, I sware unto thee, and entered into a covenant with thee, saith the Lord God, and thou becamest mine. Then washed I thee with water; yea, I throughly washed away thy blood from thee, and I anointed thee with oil. I clothed thee also with broidered work, and shod thee with badgers' skin, and I girded thee about with fine linen, and I covered thee with silk. I decked thee also with ornaments, and I put bracelets upon thy hands, and a chain on thy neck. And I put a jewel on thy forehead, and earrings in thine ears, and a beautiful crown upon thine head. Thus wast thou decked with gold and silver; and thy raiment was of fine linen, and silk, and broidered work; thou didst eat fine flour, and honey, and oil: and thou wast exceeding beautiful, and thou didst prosper into a kingdom. And thy renown went forth among the heathen for thy beauty: for it was perfect through my comeliness, which I had put upon thee, saith the Lord God.

"But thou didst trust in thine own beauty, and playedst the harlot because of thy renown, and pouredst out thy fornications on every one that passed by; his it was. And of thy garments thou didst take, and deckedst thy high places with divers colours, and playedst the harlot thereupon: the like things shall not come, neither shall it be so. Thou hast also taken thy fair jewels of my gold and of my silver, which I had given thee, and madest to thyself images of men, and didst commit whoredom with them, and tookest thy broidered garments, and coveredst them: and thou hast set mine oil and mine incense before them. My meat also which I gave thee, fine flour, and oil, and honey, wherewith I fed thee, thou hast even set it before them for a sweet savour: and thus it was, saith the Lord God. Moreover thou hast taken thy sons and thy daughters, whom thou hast borne unto me, and these hast thou sacrificed unto them to be devoured. Is this of thy whoredoms a small matter, that thou hast slain my children, and delivered them to cause them to pass through the fire for them? And in all thine abominations and thy whoredoms thou hast not remembered the days of thy youth, when thou wast naked and bare, and wast polluted in thy blood.

"And it came to pass after all thy wickedness, (woe, woe unto thee! saith the Lord God,) that thou hast also built unto thee an eminent place, and hast made thee an high place in every street. Thou hast built thy high place at every head of the way, and hast made thy beauty to be abhorred, and hast opened thy feet to every one that passed by, and multiplied thy whoredoms. Thou hast also committed fornication with the Egyptians thy neighbours, great of flesh; and hast increased thy whoredoms, to provoke me to anger. Behold, therefore I have stretched out my hand over thee, and have diminished thine ordinary food, and delivered thee unto the will of them that hate thee, the daughters of the Philistines, which are ashamed of thy lewd way.

"Thou hast played the whore also with the Assyrians, because thou wast unsatiable; yea, thou hast played the harlot with them, and yet couldest not be satisfied. Thou hast moreover multiplied thy fornication in the land of Canaan unto Chaldea; and yet thou wast not satisfied herewith. How weak is thine heart, saith the Lord God, seeing thou doest all these things, the work of an imperious whorish woman; in that thou buildest thine eminent place in the head of every way, and makest thine high place in every street; and hast not been as an harlot, in that thou scornest hire; but as a wife that committeth adultery, which taketh strangers instead of her husband! They give gifts to all whores: but thou givest thy gifts to all thy lovers, and hirest them, that they may come unto thee on every side for thy whoredom. And the contrary is in thee from other women in thy whoredoms, whereas none followeth thee to commit whoredoms: and in that thou givest a reward, and no reward is given unto thee, therefore thou art contrary.

"Wherefore, O harlot, hear the word of the Lord. Thus saith the Lord God; Because thy filthiness was poured out, and thy nakedness discovered through thy whoredoms with thy lovers, and with all the idols of thy abominations, and by the blood of thy children, which thou didst give unto them; behold, therefore I will gather all thy lovers, with whom thou hast taken pleasure, and all them that thou hast loved, with all them that thou hast hated; I will even gather them round about against thee, and will discover thy nakedness unto them, that they may see all thy nakedness. And I will judge thee, as women that break wedlock and shed blood are judged; and I will give thee blood in fury and jealousy. And I will also give thee into their hand, and they shall throw down thine eminent place, and shall break down thy high places: they shall strip thee also of thy clothes, and shall take thy fair jewels, and leave thee naked and bare. They shall also bring up a company against thee, and they shall stone thee with stones, and thrust thee through with their swords. And they shall burn thine houses with fire, and execute judgments upon thee in the sight of many women: and I will cause thee to cease from playing the harlot, and thou also shalt give no hire any more. So will

I make my fury toward thee to rest, and my jealousy shall depart from thee, and I will be quiet, and will be no more angry. Because thou hast not remembered the days of thy youth, but hast fretted me in all these things; behold, therefore I also will recompense thy way upon thine head, saith the Lord God: and thou shalt not commit this lewdness above all thine abominations.

"Behold, every one that useth proverbs shall use this proverb against thee, saying, As is the mother, so is her daughter. Thou art thy mother's daughter, that loatheth her husband and her children; and thou art the sister of thy sisters, which loathed their husbands and their children: your mother was an Hittite, and your father an Amorite. And thine elder sister is Samaria, she and her daughters that dwell at thy left hand: and thy younger sister, that dwelleth at thy right hand, is Sodom and her daughters. Yet hast thou not walked after their ways, nor done after their abominations: but, as if that were a very little thing, thou wast corrupted more than they in all thy ways.

"As I live, saith the Lord God, Sodom thy sister hath not done, she nor her daughters, as thou hast done, thou and thy daughters. Behold, this was the iniquity of thy sister Sodom, pride, fulness of bread, and abundance of idleness was in her and in her daughters, neither did she strengthen the hand of the poor and needy. And they were haughty, and committed abomination before me: therefore I took them away as I saw good. Neither hath Samaria committed half of thy sins; but thou hast multiplied thine abominations more than they, and hast justified thy sisters in all thine abominations which thou hast done. Thou also, which hast judged thy sisters, bear thine own shame for thy sins that thou hast committed more abominable than they: they are more righteous than thou: yea, be thou confounded also, and bear thy shame, in that thou hast justified thy sisters.

"When I shall bring again their captivity, the captivity of Sodom and her daughters, and the captivity of Samaria and her daughters, then will I bring again the captivity of thy captives in the midst of them: that thou mayest bear thine own shame, and mayest be confounded in all that thou hast done, in that thou art a comfort unto them. When thy sisters, Sodom and her daughters, shall return to their former estate, and Samaria and her daughters shall return to their former estate, then thou and thy daughters shall return to your former estate. For thy sister Sodom was not mentioned by thy mouth in the day of thy pride, before thy wickedness was discovered, as at the time of thy reproach of the daughters of Syria, and all that are round about her, the daughters of the Philistines, which despise thee round about.

"Thou hast borne thy lewdness and thine abominations, saith the Lord. For thus saith the Lord God; I will even deal with thee as thou hast done, which hast despised the oath in breaking the covenant. Nevertheless I will remember my covenant with thee in the days of thy youth, and I will establish unto thee an everlasting covenant. Then thou shalt remember thy ways, and be ashamed, when thou shalt receive thy sisters, thine elder and thy younger: and I will give them unto thee for daughters, but not by thy covenant. And I will establish my covenant with thee; and thou shalt know that I am the Lord: that thou mayest remember, and be confounded, and never open thy mouth any more because of thy shame, when I am pacified toward thee for all that thou hast done, saith the Lord God."

And the word of the Lord came unto me, saying,

"Son of man, put forth a riddle, and speak a parable unto the house of Israel; and say, Thus saith the Lord God; A great eagle with great wings, longwinged, full of feathers, which had divers colours, came unto Lebanon, and took the highest branch of the cedar: he cropped off the top of his young twigs, and carried it into a land of traffic; he set it in a city of merchants.

He took also of the seed of the land, and planted it in a fruitful field; he placed it by great waters, and set it as a willow tree. And it grew, and became a spreading vine of low stature, whose branches turned toward him, and the roots thereof were under him: so it became a vine, and brought forth branches, and shot forth sprigs. There was also another great eagle with great wings and many feathers: and, behold, this vine did bend her roots toward him, and shot forth her branches toward him, that he might water it by the furrows of her plantation. It was planted in a good soil by great waters, that it might bring forth branches, and that it might bear fruit, that it might be a goodly vine. Say thou, Thus saith the Lord God; Shall it prosper? shall he not pull up the roots thereof, and cut off the fruit thereof, that it wither? it shall wither in all the leaves of her spring, even without great power or many people to pluck it up by the roots thereof. Yea, behold, being planted, shall it prosper? shall it not utterly wither, when the east wind toucheth it? it shall wither in the furrows where it grew."

Moreover the word of the Lord came unto me, saying,

"Say now to the rebellious house, Know ye not what these things mean? tell them, Behold, the king of Babylon is come to Jerusalem, and hath taken the king thereof, and the princes thereof, and led them with him to Babylon; and hath taken of the king's seed, and made a covenant with him, and hath taken an oath of him: he hath also taken the mighty of the land: that the kingdom might be base, that it might not lift itself up, but that by keeping of his covenant it might stand. But he rebelled against him in sending his ambassadors into Egypt, that they might give him horses and much people. Shall he prosper? shall he escape that doeth such things? or shall he break the covenant, and be delivered? As I live, saith the Lord God, surely in the place where the king dwelleth that made him king, whose oath he despised, and whose covenant he brake, even with him in the midst of Babylon he shall die.

"Neither shall Pharaoh with his mighty army and great company make for him in the war, by casting up mounts, and building forts, to cut off many persons: seeing he despised the oath by breaking the covenant, when, lo, he had given his hand, and hath done all these things, he shall not escape. Therefore thus saith the Lord God; As I live, surely mine oath that he hath despised, and my covenant that he hath broken, even it will I recompense upon his own head. And I will spread my net upon him, and he shall be taken in my snare, and I will bring him to Babylon, and will plead with him there for his trespass that he hath trespassed against me.

And all his fugitives with all his bands shall fall by the sword, and they that remain shall be scattered toward all winds: and ye shall know that I the Lord have spoken it.

"Thus saith the Lord God; I will also take of the highest branch of the high cedar, and will set it; I will crop off from the top of his young twigs a tender one, and will plant it upon an high mountain and eminent: in the mountain of the height of Israel will I plant it: and it shall bring forth boughs, and bear fruit, and be a goodly cedar: and under it shall dwell all fowl of every wing; in the shadow of the branches thereof shall they dwell. And all the trees of the field shall know that I the Lord have brought down the high tree, have exalted the low tree, have dried up the green tree, and have made the dry tree to flourish: I the Lord have spoken and have done it."

The word of the Lord came unto me again, saying,

"What mean ye, that ye use this proverb concerning the land of Israel, saying, The fathers have eaten sour grapes, and the children's teeth are set on edge? As I live, saith the Lord God, ye shall not have occasion any more to use this proverb in Israel. Behold, all souls are mine; as the soul of the father, so also the soul of the son is mine: the soul that sinneth, it shall die.

"But if a man be just, and do that which is lawful and right, and hath not eaten upon the mountains, neither hath lifted up his eyes to the idols of the house of Israel, neither hath defiled his neighbour's wife, neither hath come near to a menstruous woman, and hath not oppressed any, but hath restored to the debtor his pledge, hath spoiled none by violence, hath given his bread to the hungry, and hath covered the naked with a garment; he that hath not given forth upon usury, neither hath taken any increase, that hath withdrawn his hand from iniquity, hath executed true judgment between man and man, hath walked in my statutes, and hath kept my judgments, to deal truly; he is just, he shall surely live, saith the Lord God.

"If he beget a son that is a robber, a shedder of blood, and that doeth the like to any one of these things, and that doeth not any of those duties, but even hath eaten upon the mountains, and defiled his neighbour's wife, hath oppressed the poor and needy, hath spoiled by violence, hath not restored the pledge, and hath lifted up his eyes to the idols, hath committed abomination, hath given forth upon usury, and hath taken increase: shall he then live? he shall not live: he hath done all these abominations; he shall surely die; his blood shall be upon him.

"Now, lo, if he beget a son, that seeth all his father's sins which he hath done, and considereth, and doeth not such like, that hath not eaten upon the mountains, neither hath lifted up his eyes to the idols of the house of Israel, hath not defiled his neighbour's wife, neither hath oppressed any, hath not withholden the pledge, neither hath spoiled by violence, but hath given his bread to the hungry, and hath covered the naked with a garment; that hath taken off his hand from the poor, that hath not received usury nor increase, hath executed my judgments, hath walked in my statutes; he shall not die for the iniquity of his father, he shall surely live.

"As for his father, because he cruelly oppressed, spoiled his brother by violence, and did that which is not good among his people, lo, even he shall die in his iniquity. Yet say ye, Why? doth not the son bear the iniquity of the father? When the son hath done that which is lawful and right, and hath kept all my statutes, and hath done them, he shall surely live. The soul that sinneth, it shall die. The son shall not bear the iniquity of the father, neither shall the father bear the iniquity of the son: the righteousness of the righteous shall be upon him, and the wickedness of the wicked shall be upon him.

"But if the wicked will turn from all his sins that he hath committed, and keep all my statutes, and do that which is lawful and right, he shall surely live, he shall not die. All his transgressions that he hath committed, they shall not be mentioned unto him: in his righteousness that he hath done he shall live. Have I any pleasure at all that the wicked should die? saith the Lord God: and not that he should return from his ways and live? But when the righteous turneth away from his righteousness, and committeth iniquity, and doeth according to all the abominations that the wicked man doeth, shall he live? All his righteousness that he hath done shall not be mentioned: in his trespass that he hath trespassed, and in his sin that he hath sinned, in them shall he die.

"Yet ye say, The way of the Lord is not equal. Hear now, O house of Israel; is not my way equal? are not your ways unequal? When a righteous man turneth away from his righteousness, and committeth iniquity, and dieth in them; for his iniquity that he hath done shall he die. Again, when the wicked man turneth away from his wickedness that he hath committed, and doeth that which is lawful and right, he shall save his soul alive. Because he considereth, and turneth away from all his transgressions that he hath committed, he shall surely live, he shall not die.

"Yet saith the house of Israel, The way of the Lord is not equal. O house of Israel, are not my ways equal? are not your ways unequal?

Therefore I will judge you, O house of Israel, every one according to his ways, saith the Lord God. Repent, and turn yourselves from all your transgressions; so iniquity shall not be your ruin. Cast away from you all your transgressions, whereby ye have transgressed; and make you a new heart and a new spirit: for why will ye die, O house of Israel? For I have no pleasure in the death of him that dieth, saith the Lord God: wherefore turn yourselves, and live ye.

"Moreover take thou up a lamentation for the princes of Israel, and say, What is thy mother? A lioness: she lay down among lions, she nourished her whelps among young lions. And she brought up one of her whelps: it became a young lion, and it learned to catch the prey; it devoured men. The nations also heard of him; he was taken in their pit, and they brought him with chains unto the land of Egypt. Now when she saw that she had waited, and her hope was lost, then she took another of her whelps, and made him a young lion. And he went up and down among the lions, he became a young lion, and learned to catch the prey, and devoured men. And he knew their desolate palaces, and he laid waste their cities; and the land was desolate, and the fulness thereof, by the noise of his roaring. Then the nations set against him on every side from the provinces, and spread their net over him: he was taken in their pit. And they put him in ward in chains, and brought him to the king of Babylon: they brought him into holds, that his voice should no more be heard upon the mountains of Israel.

"Thy mother is like a vine in thy blood, planted by the waters: she was fruitful and full of branches by reason of many waters. And she had strong rods for the sceptres of them that bare rule, and her stature was exalted among the thick branches, and she appeared in her height with the multitude of her branches. But she was plucked up in fury, she was cast down to the ground, and the east wind dried up her fruit: her strong rods were broken and withered; the fire consumed them. And now she is planted in the wilderness, in a dry and thirsty ground. And fire is gone out of a rod of her branches, which hath devoured her fruit, so that she hath no strong rod to be a sceptre to rule. This is a lamentation, and shall be for a lamentation."

And it came to pass in the seventh year, in the fifth month, the tenth day of the month, that certain of the elders of Israel came to enquire of the Lord, and sat before me. Then came the word of the Lord unto me, saying,

"Son of man, speak unto the elders of Israel, and say unto them, Thus saith the Lord God;

Are ye come to enquire of me? As I live, saith the Lord God, I will not be enquired of by you.

"Wilt thou judge them, son of man, wilt thou judge them? cause them to know the abominations of their fathers: and say unto them, Thus saith the Lord God; In the day when I chose Israel, and lifted up mine hand unto the seed of the house of Jacob, and made myself known unto them in the land of Egypt, when I lifted up mine hand unto them, saying, I am the Lord your God; in the day that I lifted up mine hand unto them, to bring them forth of the land of Egypt into a land that I had espied for them, flowing with milk and honey, which is the glory of all lands: then said I unto them, Cast ye away every man the abominations of his eyes, and defile not yourselves with the idols of Egypt: I am the Lord your God. But they rebelled against me, and would not hearken unto me: they did not every man cast away the abominations of their eyes, neither did they forsake the idols of Egypt. Then I said, I will pour out my fury upon them, to accomplish my anger against them in the midst of the land of Egypt. But I wrought for my name's sake, that it should not be polluted before the heathen, among whom they were, in whose sight I made myself known unto them, in bringing them forth out of the land of Egypt.

"Wherefore I caused them to go forth out of the land of Egypt, and brought them into the wilderness. And I gave them my statutes, and shewed them my judgments, which if a man do, he shall even live in them. Moreover also I gave them my sabbaths, to be a sign between me and them, that they might know that I am the Lord that sanctify them. But the house of Israel rebelled against me in the wilderness: they walked not in my statutes, and they despised my judgments, which if a man do, he shall even live in them; and my sabbaths they greatly polluted. Then I said, I would pour out my fury upon them in the wilderness, to consume them. But I wrought for my name's sake, that it should not be polluted before the heathen, in whose sight I brought them out.

"Yet also I lifted up my hand unto them in the wilderness, that I would not bring them into the land which I had given them, flowing with milk and honey, which is the glory of all lands; because they despised my judgments, and walked not in my statutes, but polluted my sabbaths: for their heart went after their idols. Nevertheless mine eye spared them from destroying them, neither did I make an end of them in the wilderness. But I said unto their children in the wilderness, Walk ye not in the statutes of your fathers, neither observe their judgments, nor defile yourselves with their idols:

I am the Lord your God; walk in my statutes, and keep my judgments, and do them; and hallow my sabbaths; and they shall be a sign between me and you, that ye may know that I am the Lord your God. Notwithstanding the children rebelled against me: they walked not in my statutes, neither kept my judgments to do them, which if a man do, he shall even live in them; they polluted my sabbaths. Then I said, I would pour out my fury upon them, to accomplish my anger against them in the wilderness. Nevertheless I withdrew mine hand, and wrought for my name's sake, that it should not be polluted in the sight of the heathen, in whose sight I brought them forth.

"I lifted up mine hand unto them also in the wilderness, that I would scatter them among the heathen, and disperse them through the countries; because they had not executed my judgments, but had despised my statutes, and had polluted my sabbaths, and their eyes were after their fathers' idols. Wherefore I gave them also statutes that were not good, and judgments whereby they should not live; and I polluted them in their own gifts, in that they caused to pass through the fire all that openeth the womb, that I might make them desolate, to the end that they might know that I am the Lord.

"Therefore, son of man, speak unto the house

of Israel, and say unto them, Thus saith the Lord God; Yet in this your fathers have blasphemed me, in that they have committed a trespass against me. For when I had brought them into the land, for the which I lifted up mine hand to give it to them, then they saw every high hill, and all the thick trees, and they offered there their sacrifices, and there they presented the provocation of their offering: there also they made their sweet savour, and poured out there their drink offerings. Then I said unto them, What is the high place whereunto ye go? And the name thereof is called Bamah unto this day.

"Wherefore say unto the house of Israel, Thus saith the Lord God; Are ye polluted after the manner of your fathers? and commit ye whoredom after their abominations? for when ye offer your gifts, when ye make your sons to pass through the fire, ye pollute yourselves with all your idols, even unto this day: and shall I be enquired of by you, O house of Israel? As I live, saith the Lord God, I will not be enquired of by you. And that which cometh into your mind shall not be at all, that ye say, We will be as the heathen, as the families of the countries, to serve wood and stone. As I live, saith the Lord God, surely with a mighty hand, and with a stretched out arm, and with fury poured out, will I rule over you: and I will bring you out from the people, and will gather you out of the countries wherein ye are scattered, with a mighty hand, and with a stretched out arm, and with fury poured out. And I will bring you into the wilderness of the people, and there will I plead with you face to face. Like as I pleaded with your fathers in the wilderness of the land of Egypt, so will I plead with you, saith the Lord God. And I will cause you to pass under the rod, and I will bring you into the bond of the covenant: and I will purge out from among you the rebels, and them that transgress against me: I will bring them forth out of the country where they sojourn, and they shall not enter into the land of Israel: and ye shall know that I am the Lord.

"As for you, O house of Israel, thus saith the Lord God; Go ye, serve ye every one his idols, and hereafter also, if ye will not hearken unto me: but pollute ye my holy name no more with your gifts, and with your idols. For in mine holy mountain, in the mountain of the height of Israel, saith the Lord God, there shall all the house of Israel, all of them in the land, serve me: there will I accept them, and there will I require your offerings, and the firstfruits of your oblations, with all your holy things. I will accept you with your sweet savour, when I bring you out from the people, and gather you out of the countries wherein ye have been scattered; and I will be sanctified in you before the heathen. And ye shall know that I am the Lord, when I shall bring you into the land of Israel, into the country for the which I lifted up mine hand to give it to your fathers. And there shall ye remember your ways, and all your doings, wherein ye have been defiled; and ye shall loathe yourselves in your own sight for all your evils that ye have committed. And ye shall know that I am the Lord, when I have wrought with you for my name's sake, not according to your wicked ways, nor according to your corrupt doings, O ye house of Israel, saith the Lord God."

Moreover the word of the Lord came unto me, saying,

"Son of man, set thy face toward the south, and drop thy word toward the south, and prophesy against the forest of the south field; and say to the forest of the south, Hear the word of the Lord; thus saith the Lord God; Behold, I will kindle a fire in thee, and it shall devour every green tree in thee, and every dry tree: the flaming flame shall not be quenched, and all faces from the south to the north shall be burned therein. And all flesh shall see that I the Lord have kindled it: it shall not be quenched."

Then said I, "Ah Lord God! they say of me, Doth he not speak parables?"

And the word of the Lord came unto me, saying,

"Son of man, set thy face toward Jerusalem, and drop thy word toward the holy places, and prophesy against the land of Israel, and say to the land of Israel, Thus saith the Lord; Behold, I am against thee, and will draw forth my sword out of his sheath, and will cut off from thee the righteous and the wicked. Seeing then that I will cut off from thee the righteous and the wicked, therefore shall my sword go forth out of his sheath against all flesh from the south to the north: that all flesh may know that I the Lord have drawn forth my sword out of his sheath: it shall not return any more.

"Sigh therefore, thou son of man, with the breaking of thy loins; and with bitterness sigh before their eyes. And it shall be, when they say unto thee, Wherefore sighest thou? that thou shalt answer, For the tidings; because it cometh: and every heart shall melt, and all hands shall be feeble, and every spirit shall faint, and all knees shall be weak as water: behold, it cometh, and shall be brought to pass, saith the Lord God."

Again the word of the Lord came unto me, saying,

"Son of man, prophesy, and say, Thus saith the Lord; Say, A sword, a sword is sharpened, and also furbished: it is sharpened to make a sore slaughter; it is furbished that it may glitter: should we then make mirth? it contemneth the rod of my son, as every tree. And he hath given it to be furbished, that it may be handled: this sword is sharpened, and it is furbished, to give it into the hand of the slayer. Cry and howl, son of man: for it shall be upon my people, it shall be upon all the princes of Israel: terrors by reason of the sword shall be upon my people: smite therefore upon thy thigh. Because it is a trial, and what if the sword contemn even the rod? it shall be no more, saith the Lord God. Thou therefore, son of man, prophesy, and smite thine hands together, and let the sword be doubled the third time, the sword of the slain: it is the sword of the great men that are slain, which entereth into their privy chambers. I have set the point of the sword against all their gates, that their heart may faint, and their ruins be multiplied: ah! it is made bright, it is wrapped up for the slaughter. Go thee one way or other, either on the right hand, or on the left, whithersoever thy face is set. I will also smite mine hands together, and I will cause my fury to rest: I the Lord have said it."

The word of the Lord came unto me again, saying,

"Also, thou son of man, appoint thee two ways, that the sword of the king of Babylon may come: both twain shall come forth out of one land: and choose thou a place, choose it at the head of the way to the city. Appoint a way, that the sword may come to Rabbath of the Ammonites, and to Judah in Jerusalem the defenced. For the king of Babylon stood at the parting of the way, at the head of the two ways, to use divination: he made his arrows bright, he consulted with images, he looked in the liver. At his right hand was the divination for Jerusalem, to appoint captains, to open the mouth in the slaughter, to lift up the voice with shouting, to appoint battering rams against the gates, to cast a mount, and to build a fort. And it shall be unto them as a false divination in their sight, to them that have sworn oaths: but he will call to remembrance the iniquity, that they may be taken.

"Therefore thus saith the Lord God; Because ye have made your iniquity to be remembered, in that your transgressions are discovered, so that in all your doings your sins do appear; because, I say, that ye are come to remembrance, ye shall be taken with the hand. And thou, profane wicked prince of Israel, whose day is come, when iniquity shall have an end, thus saith the Lord God; Remove the diadem, and take off the crown: this shall not be the same: exalt him that is low, and abase him that is high. I will overturn, overturn, overturn, it:

and it shall be no more, until he come whose right it is; and I will give it him.

"And thou, son of man, prophesy and say, Thus saith the Lord God concerning the Ammonites, and concerning their reproach; even say thou, The sword, the sword is drawn: for the slaughter it is furbished, to consume because of the glittering: whiles they see vanity unto thee, whiles they divine a lie unto thee, to bring thee upon the necks of them that are slain, of the wicked, whose day is come, when their iniquity shall have an end. Shall I cause it to return into his sheath? I will judge thee in the place where thou wast created, in the land of thy nativity. And I will pour out mine indignation upon thee, I will blow against thee in the fire of my wrath, and deliver thee into the hand of brutish men, and skilful to destroy. Thou shalt be for fuel to the fire; thy blood shall be in the midst of the land; thou shalt be no more remembered: for I the Lord have spoken it."

Moreover the word of the Lord came unto me, saying,

"Now, thou son of man, wilt thou judge, wilt thou judge the bloody city? yea, thou shalt shew her all her abominations.

"Then say thou, Thus saith the Lord God, The city sheddeth blood in the midst of it, that her time may come, and maketh idols against herself to defile herself. Thou art become guilty in thy blood that thou hast shed; and hast defiled thyself in thine idols which thou hast made; and thou hast caused thy days to draw near, and art come even unto thy years: therefore have I made thee a reproach unto the heathen, and a mocking to all countries. Those that be near, and those that be far from thee, shall mock thee, which art infamous and much vexed.

"Behold, the princes of Israel, every one, were in thee to their power to shed blood. In thee have they set light by father and mother: in the midst of thee have they dealt by oppression with the stranger: in thee have they vexed the fatherless and the widow. Thou hast despised mine holy things, and hast profaned my sabbaths. In thee are men that carry tales to shed blood: and in thee they eat upon the mountains: in the midst of thee they commit lewdness. In thee have they discovered their fathers' nakedness: in thee have they humbled her that was set apart for pollution. And one hath committed abomination with his neighbour's wife; and another hath lewdly defiled his daughter in law; and another in thee hath humbled his sister, his father's daughter. In thee have they taken gifts to shed blood; thou hast taken usury and increase, and thou hast greedily gained of thy neighbours by extortion, and hast forgotten me, saith the Lord God.

"Behold, therefore I have smitten mine hand at thy dishonest gain which thou hast made, and at thy blood which hath been in the midst of thee. Can thine heart endure, or can thine hands be strong, in the days that I shall deal with thee? I the Lord have spoken it, and will do it. And I will scatter thee among the heathen, and disperse thee in the countries, and will consume thy filthiness out of thee. And thou shalt take thine inheritance in thyself in the sight of the heathen, and thou shalt know that I am the Lord."

And the word of the Lord came unto me, saying,

"Son of man, the house of Israel is to me become dross: all they are brass, and tin, and iron, and lead, in the midst of the furnace; they are even the dross of silver. Therefore thus saith the Lord God; Because ye are all become dross, behold, therefore I will gather you into the midst of Jerusalem. As they gather silver, and brass, and iron, and lead, and tin, into the midst of the furnace, to blow the fire upon it, to melt it; so will I gather you in mine anger and in my fury, and I will leave you there, and melt you. Yea, I will gather you, and blow upon you in the fire of my wrath, and ye shall be melted in the midst thereof. As silver is melted in the midst of the furnace, so shall ye be melted in the midst thereof; and ye shall know that I the Lord have poured out my fury upon you."

And the word of the Lord came unto me, saying,

"Son of man, say unto her, Thou art the land that is not cleansed, nor rained upon in the day of indignation. There is a conspiracy of her prophets in the midst thereof, like a roaring lion ravening the prey; they have devoured souls; they have taken the treasure and precious things; they have made her many widows in the midst thereof. Her priests have violated my law, and have profaned mine holy things: they have put no difference between the holy and profane, neither have they shewed difference between the unclean and the clean, and have hid their eyes from my sabbaths, and I am profaned among them. Her princes in the midst thereof are like wolves ravening the prey, to shed blood, and to destroy souls, to get dishonest gain. And her prophets have daubed them with untempered mortar, seeing vanity, and divining lies unto them, saying, Thus saith the Lord God, when the Lord hath not spoken. The people of the land have used oppression, and exercised robbery, and have vexed the poor and needy: yea, they have oppressed the stranger wrongfully. And I sought for a man among them, that should make up the hedge, and stand in the gap before me for the land, that I should not destroy it: but I found none. Therefore have I poured out mine indignation upon them; I have consumed them with the fire of my wrath: their own way have I recompensed upon their heads, saith the Lord God."

The word of the Lord came again unto me, saying,

"Son of man, there were two women, the daughters of one mother: and they committed whoredoms in Egypt; they committed whoredoms in their youth: there were their breasts pressed, and there they bruised the teats of their virginity. And the names of them were Aholah the elder, and Aholibah her sister: and they were mine, and they bare sons and daughters. Thus were their names; Samaria is Aholah, and Jerusalem Aholibah.

"And Aholah played the harlot when she was mine; and she doted on her lovers, on the Assyrians her neighbours, which were clothed with blue, captains and rulers, all of them desirable young men, horsemen riding upon horses. Thus she committed her whoredoms with them, with all them that were the chosen men of Assyria, and with all on whom she doted: with all their idols she defiled herself. Neither left she her whoredoms brought from Egypt: for in her youth they lay with her, and they bruised the breasts of her virginity, and poured their whoredom upon her. Wherefore I have delivered her into the hand of her lovers, into the hand of the Assyrians, upon whom she doted. These discovered her nakedness: they took her sons and her daughters, and slew her with the sword: and she became famous among women; for they had executed judgment upon her.

"And when her sister Aholibah saw this, she was more corrupt in her inordinate love than she, and in her whoredoms more than her sister in her whoredoms. She doted upon the Assyrians her neighbours, captains and rulers clothed most gorgeously, horsemen riding upon horses, all of them desirable young men. Then I saw that she was defiled, that they took both one way, and that she increased her whoredoms: for when she saw men portrayed upon the wall, the images of the Chaldeans portrayed with vermilion, girded with girdles upon their loins, exceeding in dyed attire upon their heads, all of them princes to look to, after the manner of the Babylonians of Chaldea, the land of their nativity: and as soon as she saw them with her eyes, she doted upon them, and sent messengers unto them into Chaldea. And the Babylonians came to her into the bed of love, and they defiled her with their whoredom, and she was polluted with them, and her mind was alienated from them. So she discovered her whoredoms, and discovered her nakedness: then my mind was alienated from her, like as my mind was alienated from her sister. Yet she multiplied her whoredoms, in calling to remembrance the days of her youth, wherein she had played the harlot in the land of Egypt. For she doted upon their paramours, whose flesh is as the flesh of asses, and whose issue is like the issue of horses. Thus thou calledst to remembrance the lewdness of thy youth, in bruising thy teats by the Egyptians for the paps of thy youth.

"Therefore, O Aholibah, thus saith the Lord God; Behold, I will raise up thy lovers against thee, from whom thy mind is alienated, and I will bring them against thee on every side; the Babylonians, and all the Chaldeans, Pekod, and Shoa, and Koa, and all the Assyrians with them: all of them desirable young men, captains and rulers, great lords and renowned, all of them riding upon horses. And they shall come against thee with chariots, wagons, and wheels, and with an assembly of people, which shall set against thee buckler and shield and helmet round about: and I will set judgment before them, and they shall judge thee according to their judgments. And I will set my jealousy against thee, and they shall deal furiously with thee: they shall take away thy nose and thine ears; and thy remnant shall fall by the sword: they shall take thy sons and thy daughters; and thy residue shall be devoured by the fire. They shall also strip thee out of thy clothes, and take away thy fair jewels. Thus will I make thy lewdness to cease from thee, and thy whoredom brought from the land of Egypt: so that thou shalt not lift up thine eyes unto them, nor remember Egypt any more. For thus saith the Lord God; Behold, I will deliver thee into the hand of them whom thou hatest, into the hand of them from whom thy mind is alienated: and they shall deal with thee hatefully, and shall take away all thy labour, and shall leave thee naked and bare: and the nakedness of thy whoredoms shall be discovered, both thy lewdness and thy whoredoms. I will do these things unto thee, because thou hast gone a whoring after the heathen, and because thou art polluted with their idols. Thou hast walked in the way of thy sister; therefore will I give her cup into thine hand.

"Thus saith the Lord God; Thou shalt drink of thy sister's cup deep and large: thou shalt be laughed to scorn and had in derision; it containeth much. Thou shalt be filled with drunkenness and sorrow, with the cup of astonishment and desolation, with the cup of thy sister Samaria. Thou shalt even drink it and suck it out, and thou shalt break the sherds thereof, and pluck off thine own breasts: for I have spoken it, saith the Lord God. Therefore thus saith the Lord God; Because thou hast forgotten me, and cast me behind thy back, therefore bear thou also thy lewdness and thy whoredoms."

The Lord said moreover unto me, "Son of man, wilt thou judge Aholah and Aholibah? yea, declare unto them their abominations; that they have committed adultery, and blood is in their hands, and with their idols have they committed adultery, and have also caused their sons, whom they bare unto me, to pass for them through the fire, to devour them.

"Moreover this they have done unto me: they have defiled my sanctuary in the same day, and have profaned my sabbaths. For when they had slain their children to their idols, then they came the same day into my sanctuary to profane it; and, lo, thus have they done in the midst of mine house.

"And furthermore, that ye have sent for men to come from far, unto whom a messenger was sent; and, lo, they came: for whom thou didst wash thyself, paintedst thy eyes, and deckedst thyself with ornaments, and satest upon a stately bed, and a table prepared before it, whereupon thou hast set mine incense and mine oil. And a voice of a multitude being at ease was with her: and with the men of the common sort were brought Sabeans from the wilderness, which put bracelets upon their hands, and beautiful crowns upon their heads.

"Then said I unto her that was old in adulteries, Will they now commit whoredoms with her, and she with them? Yet they went in unto her, as they go in unto a woman that playeth the harlot: so went they in unto Aholah and unto Aholibah, the lewd women. And the righteous men, they shall judge them after the manner of adulteresses, and after the manner of women that shed blood; because they are adulteresses, and blood is in their hands.

"For thus saith the Lord God; I will bring up a company upon them, and will give them to be removed and spoiled. And the company shall stone them with stones, and dispatch them with their swords; they shall slay their sons and their daughters, and burn up their houses with fire. Thus will I cause lewdness to cease out of the land, that all women may be taught not to do after your lewdness. And they shall recompense your lewdness upon you, and ye shall bear the sins of your idols: and ye shall know that I am the Lord God."

Again in the ninth year, in the tenth month, in the tenth day of the month, the word of the Lord came unto me, saying,

"Son of man, write thee the name of the day, even of this same day: the king of Babylon set himself against Jerusalem this same day.

"And utter a parable unto the rebellious house, and say unto them, Thus saith the Lord

God; Set on a pot, set it on, and also pour water into it: gather the pieces thereof into it, even every good piece, the thigh, and the shoulder; fill it with the choice bones. Take the choice of the flock, and burn also the bones under it, and make it boil well, and let them seethe the bones of it therein.

"Wherefore thus saith the Lord God; Woe to the bloody city, to the pot whose scum is therein, and whose scum is not gone out of it! bring it out piece by piece; let no lot fall upon it. For her blood is in the midst of her; she set it upon the top of a rock; she poured it not upon the ground, to cover it with dust; that it might cause fury to come up to take vengeance; I have set her blood upon the top of a rock, that it should not be covered. Therefore thus saith the Lord God; Woe to the bloody city! I will even make the pile for fire great. Heap on wood, kindle the fire, consume the flesh, and spice it well, and let the bones be burned. Then set it empty upon the coals thereof, that the brass of it may be hot, and may burn, and that the filthiness of it may be molten in it, that the scum of it may be consumed. She hath wearied herself with lies, and her great scum went not forth out of her: her scum shall be in the fire. In thy filthiness is lewdness: because I have purged thee, and thou wast not purged, thou shalt not be purged from thy filthiness any more, till I have caused my fury to rest upon thee. I the Lord have spoken it: it shall come to pass, and I will do it; I will not go back, neither will I spare, neither will I repent ; according to thy ways, and according to thy doings, shall they judge thee, saith the Lord God."

Also the word of the Lord came unto me, saying,

"Son of man, behold, I take away from thee the desire of thine eyes with a stroke: yet neither shalt thou mourn nor weep, neither shall thy tears run down. Forbear to cry, make no mourning for the dead, bind the tire of thine head upon thee, and put on thy shoes upon thy feet, and cover not thy lips, and eat not the bread of men." So I spake unto the people in the morning: and at even my wife died; and I did in the morning as I was commanded. And the people said unto me, "Wilt thou not tell us what these things are to us, that thou doest so?"

Then I answered them, "The word of the Lord came unto me, saying, Speak unto the house of Israel, Thus saith the Lord God; Behold, I will profane my sanctuary, the excellency of your strength, the desire of your eyes, and that which your soul pitieth; and your sons and your daughters whom ye have left shall fall by the sword. And ye shall do as I have done: ye shall not cover your lips, nor eat the bread of men. And your tires shall be upon your heads, and your shoes upon your feet: ye shall not mourn nor weep; but ye shall pine away for your iniquities, and mourn one toward another. Thus Ezekiel is unto you a sign: according to all that he hath done shall ye do: and when this cometh, ye shall know that I am the Lord God.

"Also, thou son of man, shall it not be in the day when I take from them their strength, the joy of their glory, the desire of their eyes, and that whereupon they set their minds, their sons and their daughters, that he that escapeth in that day shall come unto thee, to cause thee to hear it with thine ears? In that day shall thy mouth be opened to him which is escaped, and thou shalt speak, and be no more dumb: and thou shalt be a sign unto them; and they shall know that I am the Lord."

The word of the Lord came again unto me, saying,

"Son of man, set thy face against the Ammonites, and prophesy against them; and say unto the Ammonites, Hear the word of the Lord God; Thus saith the Lord God; Because thou saidst, Aha, against my sanctuary, when it was profaned; and against the land of Israel, when it was desolate; and against the house of Judah, when they went into captivity; behold, therefore I will deliver thee to the men of the

East for a possession, and they shall set their palaces in thee, and make their dwellings in thee: they shall eat thy fruit, and they shall drink thy milk. And I will make Rabbah a stable for camels, and the Ammonites a couchingplace for flocks: and ye shall know that I am the Lord. For thus saith the Lord God; Because thou hast clapped thine hands, and stamped with the feet, and rejoiced in heart with all thy despite against the land of Israel; behold, therefore I will stretch out mine hand upon thee, and will deliver thee for a spoil to the heathen; and I will cut thee off from the people, and I will cause thee to perish out of the countries: I will destroy thee; and thou shalt know that I am the Lord.

"Thus saith the Lord God; Because that Moab and Seir do say, Behold, the house of Judah is like unto all the heathen; therefore, behold, I will open the side of Moab from the cities, from his cities which are on his frontiers, the glory of the country, Beth-jeshimoth, Baal-meon, and Kiriathaim, unto the men of the East with the Ammonites, and will give them in possession, that the Ammonites may not be remembered among the nations. And I will execute judgments upon Moab; and they shall know that I am the Lord.

"Thus saith the Lord God; Because that Edom hath dealt against the house of Judah by taking vengeance, and hath greatly offended, and revenged himself upon them; therefore thus saith the Lord God; I will also stretch out mine hand upon Edom, and will cut off man and beast from it; and I will make it desolate from Teman; and they of Dedan shall fall by the sword. And I will lay my vengeance upon Edom by the hand of my people Israel: and they shall do in Edom according to mine anger and according to my fury; and they shall know my vengeance, saith the Lord God.

"Thus saith the Lord God; Because the Philistines have dealt by revenge, and have taken vengeance with a despiteful heart, to destroy it for the old hatred; therefore thus saith the Lord God; Behold, I will stretch out mine hand upon the Philistines, and I will cut off the Cherethims, and destroy the remnant of the sea coast. And I will execute great vengeance upon them with furious rebukes; and they shall know that I am the Lord, when I shall lay my vengeance upon them."

And it came to pass in the eleventh year, in the first day of the month, that the word of the Lord came unto me, saying,

"Son of man, because that Tyrus hath said against Jerusalem, Aha, she is broken that was the gates of the people: she is turned unto me: I shall be replenished, now she is laid waste: therefore thus saith the Lord God; Behold, I am against thee, O Tyrus, and will cause many nations to come up against thee, as the sea causeth his waves to come up. And they shall destroy the walls of Tyrus, and break down her towers: I will also scrape her dust from her, and make her like the top of a rock. It shall be a place for the spreading of nets in the midst of the sea: for I have spoken it, saith the Lord God: and it shall become a spoil to the nations. And her daughters which are in the field shall be slain by the sword; and they shall know that I am the Lord.

"For thus saith the Lord God; Behold, I will bring upon Tyrus Nebuchadrezzar king of Babylon, a king of kings, from the north, with horses, and with chariots, and with horsemen, and companies, and much people. He shall slay with the sword thy daughters in the field: and he shall make a fort against thee, and cast a mount against thee, and lift up the buckler against thee. And he shall set engines of war against thy walls, and with his axes he shall break down thy towers. By reason of the abundance of his horses their dust shall cover thee: thy walls shall shake at the noise of the horsemen, and of the wheels, and of the chariots, when he shall enter into thy gates, as men enter into a city wherein is made a breach. With the hoofs of his horses shall he tread down all thy streets: he shall slay thy people by the sword, and thy

strong garrisons shall go down to the ground.
And they shall make a spoil of thy riches, and
make a prey of thy merchandise: and they shall
break down thy walls, and destroy thy pleasant
houses: and they shall lay thy stones and thy
timber and thy dust in the midst of the water.
And I will cause the noise of thy songs to cease;
and the sound of thy harps shall be no more
heard. And I will make thee like the top of a
rock: thou shalt be a place to spread nets upon;
thou shalt be built no more: for I the Lord have
spoken it, saith the Lord God.

"Thus saith the Lord God to Tyrus; Shall
not the isles shake at the sound of thy fall, when
the wounded cry, when the slaughter is made in
the midst of thee? Then all the princes of the
sea shall come down from their thrones, and lay
away their robes, and put off their broidered
garments: they shall clothe themselves with
trembling; they shall sit upon the ground, and
shall tremble at every moment, and be astonished
at thee. And they shall take up a lamentation
for thee, and say to thee, How art thou destroyed,
that wast inhabited of seafaring men, the renowned city, which wast strong in the sea, she
and her inhabitants, which cause their terror to
be on all that haunt it! Now shall the isles
tremble in the day of thy fall; yea, the isles
that are in the sea shall be troubled at thy
departure.

"For thus saith the Lord God; When I shall make thee a desolate city, like the cities that are not inhabited; when I shall bring up the deep upon thee, and great waters shall cover thee; when I shall bring thee down with them that descend into the pit, with the people of old time, and shall set thee in the low parts of the earth, in places desolate of old, with them that go down to the pit, that thou be not inhabited; and I shall set glory in the land of the living; I will make thee a terror, and thou shalt be no more: though thou be sought for, yet shalt thou never be found again, saith the Lord God."

The word of the Lord came again unto me, saying,

"Now, thou son of man, take up a lamentation for Tyrus; and say unto Tyrus, O thou that art situate at the entry of the sea, which art a merchant of the people for many isles, thus saith the Lord God; O Tyrus, thou hast said, I am of perfect beauty. Thy borders are in the midst of the seas, thy builders have perfected thy beauty.

"They have made all thy ship boards of fir trees of Senir: they have taken cedars from Lebanon to make masts for thee. Of the oaks of Bashan have they made thine oars; the company of the Ashurites have made thy benches of ivory, brought out of the isles of Chittim. Fine linen with broidered work from Egypt was that which thou spreadest forth to be thy sail; blue and purple from the isles of Elishah was that which covered thee. The inhabitants of Zidon and Arvad were thy mariners: thy wise men, O Tyrus, that were in thee, were thy pilots. The ancients of Gebal and the wise men thereof were in thee thy calkers: all the ships of the sea with their mariners were in thee to occupy thy merchandise.

"They of Persia and of Lud and of Phut were in thine army, thy men of war: they hanged the shield and helmet in thee; they set forth thy comeliness. The men of Arvad with thine army were upon thy walls round about, and the Gammadims were in thy towers: they hanged their shields upon thy walls round about: they have made thy beauty perfect.

"Tarshish was thy merchant by reason of the multitude of all kind of riches; with silver, iron, tin, and lead, they traded in thy fairs. Javan, Tubal, and Meshech, they were thy merchants: they traded the persons of men and vessels of brass in thy market. They of the house of Togarmah traded in thy fairs with horses and horsemen and mules. The men of Dedan were thy merchants; many isles were the merchandise of thine hand: they brought thee for a present horns of ivory and ebony.

"Syria was thy merchant by reason of the multitude of the wares of thy making: they occupied in thy fairs with emeralds, purple, and broidered work, and fine linen, and coral, and agate. Judah, and the land of Israel, they were thy merchants: they traded in thy market wheat of Minnith, and Pannag, and honey, and oil, and balm. Damascus was thy merchant in the multitude of the wares of thy making, for the multitude of all riches; in the wine of Helbon, and white wool. Dan also and Javan going to and fro occupied in thy fairs: bright iron, cassia, and calamus, were in thy market.

"Dedan was thy merchant in precious clothes for chariots. Arabia, and all the princes of Kedar, they occupied with thee in lambs, and rams, and goats: in these were they thy merchants. The merchants of Sheba and Raamah, they were thy merchants: they occupied in thy fairs with chief of all spices, and with all precious stones, and gold. Haran, and Canneh, and Eden, the merchants of Sheba, Asshur, and Chilmad, were thy merchants. These were thy merchants in all sorts of things, in blue clothes, and broidered work, and in chests of rich apparel, bound with cords, and made of cedar, among thy merchandise. The ships of Tarshish did sing of thee in thy market: and thou wast replenished, and made very glorious in the midst of the seas.

"Thy rowers have brought thee into great waters: the east wind hath broken thee in the midst of the seas. Thy riches, and thy fairs, thy merchandise, thy mariners, and thy pilots, thy calkers, and the occupiers of thy merchandise, and all thy men of war, that are in thee, and in all thy company which is in the midst of thee, shall fall into the midst of the seas in the day of thy ruin. The suburbs shall shake at the sound of the cry of thy pilots. And all that handle the oar, the mariners, and all the pilots of the sea, shall come down from their ships, they shall stand upon the land; and shall cause their voice to be heard against thee, and shall cry bitterly, and shall cast up dust upon their heads, they shall wallow themselves in the ashes: and they shall make themselves utterly bald for thee, and gird them with sackcloth, and they shall weep for thee with bitterness of heart and bitter wailing. And in their wailing they shall take up a lamentation for thee, and lament over thee, saying, What city is like Tyrus, like the destroyed in the midst of the sea?

"When thy wares went forth out of the seas, thou filledst many people; thou didst enrich the kings of the earth with the multitude of thy riches and of thy merchandise. In the time when thou shalt be broken by the seas in the depths of the waters thy merchandise and all thy company in the midst of thee shall fall. All the inhabitants of the isles shall be astonished at thee, and their kings shall be sore afraid, they shall be troubled in their countenance.

The merchants among the people shall hiss at thee; thou shalt be a terror, and never shalt be any more."

The word of the Lord came again unto me, saying,

"Son of man, say unto the prince of Tyrus, Thus saith the Lord God; Because thine heart is lifted up, and thou hast said, I am a God, I sit in the seat of God, in the midst of the seas; yet thou art a man, and not God, though thou set thine heart as the heart of God: (behold, thou art wiser than Daniel; there is no secret that they can hide from thee: with thy wisdom and with thine understanding thou hast gotten thee riches, and hast gotten gold and silver into thy treasures: by thy great wisdom and by thy traffic hast thou increased thy riches, and thine heart is lifted up because of thy riches): therefore thus saith the Lord God; Because thou hast set thine heart as the heart of God; behold, therefore I will bring strangers upon thee, the terrible of the nations: and they shall draw their swords against the beauty of thy wisdom, and they shall defile thy brightness. They shall bring thee down to the pit, and thou shalt die the deaths of them that are slain in the midst of the seas. Wilt thou yet say before him that slayeth thee, I am God? but thou shalt be a man, and no God, in the hand of him that slayeth thee. Thou shalt die the deaths of the uncircumcised by the hand of strangers: for I have spoken it, saith the Lord God."

Moreover the word of the Lord came unto me, saying,

"Son of man, take up a lamentation upon the king of Tyrus, and say unto him, Thus saith the Lord God; Thou sealest up the sum, full of wisdom, and perfect in beauty. Thou hast been in Eden the garden of God; every precious stone was thy covering, the sardius, topaz, and the diamond, the beryl, the onyx, and the jasper, the sapphire, the emerald, and the carbuncle, and gold: the workmanship of thy tabrets and of thy pipes was prepared in thee in the day that thou wast created. Thou art the anointed cherub that covereth; and I have set thee so: thou wast upon the holy mountain of God; thou hast walked up and down in the midst of the stones of fire.

"Thou wast perfect in thy ways from the day that thou wast created, till iniquity was found in thee. By the multitude of thy merchandise they have filled the midst of thee with violence, and thou hast sinned: therefore I will cast thee as profane out of the mountain of God: and I will destroy thee, O covering cherub, from the midst of the stones of fire. Thine heart was lifted up because of thy beauty, thou hast corrupted thy wisdom by reason of thy brightness: I will cast thee to the ground,

I will lay thee before kings, that they may behold thee. Thou hast defiled thy sanctuaries by the multitude of thine iniquities, by the iniquity of thy traffic; therefore will I bring forth a fire from the midst of thee, it shall devour thee, and I will bring thee to ashes upon the earth in the sight of all them that behold thee. All they that know thee among the people shall be astonished at thee: thou shalt be a terror, and never shalt thou be any more."

Again the word of the Lord came unto me, saying,

"Son of man, set thy face against Zidon, and prophesy against it, and say, Thus saith the Lord God; Behold, I am against thee, O Zidon; and I will be glorified in the midst of thee: and they shall know that I am the Lord, when I shall have executed judgments in her, and shall be sanctified in her. For I will send into her pestilence, and blood into her streets; and the wounded shall be judged in the midst of her by the sword upon her on every side; and they shall know that I am the Lord. And there shall be no more a pricking brier unto the house of Israel, nor any grieving thorn of all that are round about them, that despised them; and they shall know that I am the Lord God.

"Thus saith the Lord God; When I shall have gathered the house of Israel from the people among whom they are scattered, and shall be sanctified in them in the sight of the heathen, then shall they dwell in their land that I have given to my servant Jacob. And they shall dwell safely therein, and shall build houses, and plant vineyards; yea, they shall dwell with confidence, when I have executed judgments upon all those that despise them round about them; and they shall know that I am the Lord their God."

In the tenth year, in the tenth month, in the twelfth day of the month, the word of the Lord came unto me, saying,

"Son of man, set thy face against Pharaoh king of Egypt, and prophesy against him, and against all Egypt: speak, and say, Thus saith the Lord God; Behold, I am against thee, Pharaoh king of Egypt, the great dragon that lieth in the midst of his rivers, which hath said, My river is mine own, and I have made it for myself. But I will put hooks in thy jaws, and I will cause the fish of thy rivers to stick unto thy scales, and I will bring thee up out of the midst of thy rivers, and all the fish of thy rivers shall stick unto thy scales. And I will leave thee thrown into the wilderness, thee and all the fish of thy rivers: thou shalt fall upon the open fields; thou shalt not be brought together, nor gathered: I have given thee for meat to the beasts of the field and to the fowls of the heaven.

"And all the inhabitants of Egypt shall know

that I am the Lord, because they have been a staff of reed to the house of Israel. When they took hold of thee by thy hand, thou didst break, and rend all their shoulder: and when they leaned upon thee, thou brakest, and madest all their loins to be at a stand. Therefore thus saith the Lord God; Behold, I will bring a sword upon thee, and cut off man and beast out of thee.

"And the land of Egypt shall be desolate and waste; and they shall know that I am the Lord: because he hath said, The river is mine, and I have made it. Behold, therefore I am against thee, and against thy rivers, and I will make the land of Egypt utterly waste and desolate, from the tower of Syene even unto the border of Ethiopia. No foot of man shall pass through it, nor foot of beast shall pass through it, neither shall it be inhabited forty years. And I will make the land of Egypt desolate in the midst of the countries that are desolate, and her cities among the cities that are laid waste shall be desolate forty years: and I will scatter the Egyptians among the nations, and will disperse them through the countries.

"Yet thus saith the Lord God; At the end of forty years will I gather the Egyptians from the people whither they were scattered: and I will bring again the captivity of Egypt, and will cause them to return into the land of Pathros, into the land of their habitation; and they shall be there a base kingdom. It shall be the basest of the kingdoms; neither shall it exalt itself any more above the nations: for I will diminish them, that they shall no more rule over the nations. And it shall be no more the confidence of the house of Israel, which bringeth their iniquity to remembrance, when they shall look after them: but they shall know that I am the Lord God."

And it came to pass in the seven and twentieth year, in the first month, in the first day of the month, the word of the Lord came unto me, saying,

"Son of man, Nebuchadrezzar king of Babylon caused his army to serve a great service against Tyrus: every head was made bald, and every shoulder was peeled: yet had he no wages, nor his army, for Tyrus, for the service that he had served against it. Therefore thus saith the Lord God; Behold, I will give the land of Egypt unto Nebuchadrezzar king of Babylon; and he shall take her multitude, and take her spoil, and take her prey; and it shall be the wages for his army. I have given him the land of Egypt for his labour wherewith he served against it, because they wrought for me, saith the Lord God.

"In that day will I cause the horn of the house of Israel to bud forth, and I will give thee the opening of the mouth in the midst of them; and they shall know that I am the Lord."

The word of the Lord came again unto me, saying,

"Son of man, prophesy and say, Thus saith the Lord God; Howl ye, Woe worth the day! For the day is near, even the day of the Lord is near, a cloudy day; it shall be the time of the heathen. And the sword shall come upon Egypt, and great pain shall be in Ethiopia, when the slain shall fall in Egypt, and they shall take away her multitude, and her foundations shall be broken down. Ethiopia, and Libya, and Lydia, and all the mingled people, and Chub, and the men of the land that is in league, shall fall with them by the sword.

"Thus saith the Lord; They also that uphold Egypt shall fall; and the pride of her power shall come down: from the tower of Syene shall they fall in it by the sword, saith the Lord God. And they shall be desolate in the midst of the countries that are desolate, and her cities shall be in the midst of the cities that are wasted. And they shall know that I am the Lord, when I have set a fire in Egypt, and when all her helpers shall be destroyed. In that day shall messengers go forth from me in ships to make the careless Ethiopians afraid, and great pain shall come upon them, as in the day of Egypt: for, lo, it cometh.

"Thus saith the Lord God; I will also make the multitude of Egypt to cease by the hand of Nebuchadrezzar king of Babylon. He and his people with him, the terrible of the nations, shall be brought to destroy the land: and they shall draw their swords against Egypt, and fill the land with the slain. And I will make the rivers dry, and sell the land into the hand of the wicked: and I will make the land waste, and all that is therein, by the hand of strangers: I the Lord have spoken it.

"Thus saith the Lord God; I will also destroy the idols, and I will cause their images to cease out of Noph; and there shall be no more a prince of the land of Egypt: and I will put a fear in the land of Egypt. And I will make Pathros desolate, and will set fire in Zoan, and will execute judgments in No. And I will pour my fury upon Sin, the strength of Egypt; and I will cut off the multitude of No. And I will set fire in Egypt: Sin shall have great pain, and No shall be rent asunder, and Noph shall have distresses daily. The young men of Aven and of Pi-beseth shall fall by the sword: and these cities shall go into captivity. At Tehaphnehes also the day shall be darkened, when I shall break there the yokes of Egypt: and the pomp of her strength shall cease in her: as for her, a cloud shall cover her, and her daughters shall go into captivity. Thus will I execute judgments in Egypt: and they shall know that I am the Lord."

And it came to pass in the eleventh year, in the first month, in the seventh day of the month, that the word of the Lord came unto me, saying,

"Son of man, I have broken the arm of Pharaoh king of Egypt; and, lo, it shall not be bound up to be healed, to put a roller to bind it, to make it strong to hold the sword. Therefore thus saith the Lord God; Behold, I am against Pharaoh king of Egypt, and will break his arms, the strong, and that which was broken; and I will cause the sword to fall out of his hand. And I will scatter the Egyptians among the nations, and will disperse them through the countries. And I will strengthen the arms of the king of Babylon, and put my sword in his hand: but I will break Pharaoh's arms, and he shall groan before him with the groanings of a deadly wounded man. But I will strengthen the arms of the king of Babylon, and the arms of Pharaoh shall fall down; and they shall know that I am the Lord, when I shall put my sword into the hand of the king of Babylon, and he shall stretch it out upon the land of Egypt. And I will scatter the Egyptians among the nations, and disperse them among the countries; and they shall know that I am the Lord."

And it came to pass in the eleventh year, in

the third month, in the first day of the month, that the word of the Lord came unto me, saying,

"Son of man, speak unto Pharaoh king of Egypt, and to his multitude; Whom art thou like in thy greatness?

"Behold, the Assyrian was a cedar in Lebanon with fair branches, and with a shadowing shroud, and of an high stature; and his top was among the thick boughs. The waters made him great, the deep set him up on high with her rivers running round about his plants, and sent out her little rivers unto all the trees of the field. Therefore his height was exalted above all the trees of the field, and his boughs were multiplied, and his branches became long because of the multitude of waters, when he shot forth. All the fowls of heaven made their nests in his boughs, and under his branches did all the beasts of the field bring forth their young, and under his shadow dwelt all great nations. Thus was he fair in his greatness, in the length of his branches: for his root was by great waters. The cedars in the garden of God could not hide him: the fir trees were not like his boughs, and the chesnut trees were not like his branches; nor any tree in the garden of God was like unto him in his beauty. I have made him fair by the multitude of his branches: so that all the trees of Eden, that were in the garden of God, envied him.

"Therefore thus saith the Lord God; Because thou hast lifted up thyself in height, and he hath shot up his top among the thick boughs, and his heart is lifted up in his height; I have therefore delivered him into the hand of the mighty one of the heathen; he shall surely deal with him: I have driven him out for his wickedness. And strangers, the terrible of the nations, have cut him off, and have left him: upon the mountains and in all the valleys his branches are fallen, and his boughs are broken by all the rivers of the land; and all the people of the earth are gone down from his shadow, and have left him. Upon his ruin shall all the fowls of the heaven remain, and all the beasts of the field shall be upon his branches: to the end that none of all the trees by the waters exalt themselves for their height, neither shoot up their top among the thick boughs, neither their trees stand up in their height, all that drink water: for they are all delivered unto death, to the nether parts of the earth, in the midst of the children of men, with them that go down to the pit. Thus saith the Lord God; In the day when he went down to the grave I caused a mourning: I covered the deep for him, and I restrained the floods thereof, and the great waters were stayed: and I caused Lebanon to mourn for him, and all the trees of the field fainted for him. I made the nations to shake at the sound of his fall, when I cast him down to hell with them that descend into the pit: and all the trees of Eden, the choice and best of Lebanon, all that drink water, shall be comforted in the nether parts of the earth. They also went down into hell with him unto them that be slain with the sword; and they that were his arm, that dwelt under his shadow in the midst of the heathen.

"To whom art thou thus like in glory and in greatness among the trees of Eden? yet shalt thou be brought down with the trees of Eden unto the nether parts of the earth: thou shalt lie in the midst of the uncircumcised with them that be slain by the sword. This is Pharaoh and all his multitude, saith the Lord God."

And it came to pass in the twelfth year, in the twelfth month, in the first day of the month, that the word of the Lord came unto me, saying,

"Son of man, take up a lamentation for Pharaoh king of Egypt, and say unto him, Thou art like a young lion of the nations, and thou art as a whale in the seas: and thou camest forth with thy rivers, and troubledst the waters with thy feet, and fouledst their rivers. Thus saith the Lord God; I will therefore spread out my net over thee with a company of many people; and they shall bring thee up in my net. Then will I leave thee upon the land, I will cast thee forth upon the open field, and will cause all the fowls of the heaven to remain upon thee, and I will fill the beasts of the whole earth with thee. And I will lay thy flesh upon the mountains, and fill the valleys with thy height. I will also water with thy blood the land wherein thou swimmest, even to the mountains; and the rivers shall be full of thee. And when I shall put thee out, I will cover the heaven, and make the stars thereof dark; I will cover the sun with a cloud, and the moon shall not give her light. All the bright lights of heaven will I make dark over thee, and set darkness upon thy land, saith the Lord God.

"I will also vex the hearts of many people, when I shall bring thy destruction among the nations, into the countries which thou hast not known. Yea, I will make many people amazed at thee, and their kings shall be horribly afraid for thee, when I shall brandish my sword before them; and they shall tremble at every moment, every man for his own life, in the day of thy fall. For thus saith the Lord God; The sword of the king of Babylon shall come upon thee. By the swords of the mighty will I cause thy multitude to fall, the terrible of the nations, all of them: and they shall spoil the pomp of Egypt, and all the multitude thereof shall be destroyed. I will destroy also all the beasts thereof from beside the great waters; neither shall the foot of man trouble them any more, nor the hoofs of beasts trouble them. Then will I make their waters deep, and cause their rivers to run like oil, saith the Lord God.

"When I shall make the land of Egypt desolate, and the country shall be destitute of that whereof it was full, when I shall smite all them that dwell therein, then shall they know that I am the Lord. This is the lamentation wherewith they shall lament her: the daughters of the nations shall lament her: they shall lament for her, even for Egypt, and for all her multitude, saith the Lord God."

It came to pass also in the twelfth year, in the fifteenth day of the month, that the word of the Lord came unto me, saying,

"Son of man, wail for the multitude of Egypt, and cast them down, even her, and the daughters of the famous nations, unto the nether parts of the earth, with them that go down into the pit. Whom dost thou pass in beauty? go down, and be thou laid with the uncircumcised. They shall fall in the midst of them that are slain by the sword: she is delivered to the sword: draw her and all her multitudes. The strong among the mighty shall speak to him out of the midst of hell with them that help him: they are gone down, they lie uncircumcised, slain by the sword.

"Asshur is there and all her company: his graves are about him: all of them slain, fallen by the sword: whose graves are set in the sides of the pit, and her company is round about her grave: all of them slain, fallen by the sword, which caused terror in the land of the living.

"There is Elam and all her multitude round about her grave, all of them slain, fallen by the sword, which are gone down uncircumcised into the nether parts of the earth, which caused their terror in the land of the living; yet have they borne their shame with them that go down to the pit. They have set her a bed in the midst of the slain with all her multitude: her graves are round about him: all of them uncircumcised, slain by the sword: though their terror was caused in the land of the living, yet have they borne their shame with them that go down to the pit: he is put in the midst of them that be slain.

"There is Meshech, Tubal, and all her multitude: her graves are round about him: all of them uncircumcised, slain by the sword, though they caused their terror in the land of the living. And they shall not lie with the mighty that are fallen of the uncircumcised, which are gone down to hell with their weapons of war: and they have laid their swords under their heads, but their iniquities shall be upon their bones, though they were the terror of the mighty in the land of the living. Yea, thou shalt be broken in the midst of the uncircumcised, and shalt lie with them that are slain with the sword.

"There is Edom, her kings, and all her princes, which with their might are laid by them that were slain by the sword: they shall lie with the uncircumcised, and with them that go down to the pit.

"There be the princes of the north, all of them, and all the Zidonians, which are gone down with the slain; with their terror they are ashamed of their might; and they lie uncircumcised with them that be slain by the sword, and bear their shame with them that go down to the pit. Pharaoh shall see them, and shall be comforted over all his multitude, even Pharaoh and all his army slain by the sword, saith the Lord God. For I have caused my terror in the land of the living: and he shall be laid in the midst of the uncircumcised with them that are slain with the sword, even Pharaoh and all his multitude, saith the Lord God."

Again the word of the Lord came unto me, saying,

"Son of man, speak to the children of thy people, and say unto them, When I bring the sword upon a land, if the people of the land take a man of their coasts, and set him for their watchman: if when he seeth the sword come upon the land, he blow the trumpet, and warn the people; then whosoever heareth the sound of the trumpet, and taketh not warning; if the sword come, and take him away, his blood shall be upon his own head. He heard the sound of the trumpet, and took not warning; his blood shall be upon him. But he that taketh warning shall deliver his soul. But if the watchman see the sword come, and blow not the trumpet, and the people be not warned; if the sword come, and take any person from among them, he is taken away in his iniquity; but his blood will I require at the watchman's hand.

"So thou, O son of man, I have set thee a watchman unto the house of Israel; therefore thou shalt hear the word at my mouth, and warn them from me. When I say unto the wicked, O wicked man, thou shalt surely die; if thou dost not speak to warn the wicked from his way, that wicked man shall die in his iniquity; but his blood will I require at thine hand. Nevertheless, if thou warn the wicked of his way to turn from it; if he do not turn from his way, he shall die in his iniquity; but thou hast delivered thy soul.

"Therefore, O thou son of man, speak unto the house of Israel; Thus ye speak, saying, If our transgressions and our sins be upon us, and we pine away in them, how should we then live? Say unto them, As I live, saith the Lord God, I have no pleasure in the death of the wicked; but that the wicked turn from his way and live: turn ye, turn ye from your evil ways; for why will ye die, O house of Israel?

"Therefore, thou son of man, say unto the children of thy people, The righteousness of the righteous shall not deliver him in the day of his transgression: as for the wickedness of the wicked, he shall not fall thereby in the day that he turneth from his wickedness; neither shall the righteous be able to live for his righteousness in the day that he sinneth. When I shall say to the righteous, that he shall surely live; if he trust to his own righteousness, and commit iniquity, all his righteousnesses shall not be remembered; but for his iniquity that he hath committed, he shall die for it. Again, when I say unto the wicked, Thou shalt surely die; if he turn from his sin, and do that which is lawful and right; if the wicked restore the pledge, give again that he had robbed, walk in the statutes of life, without committing iniquity; he shall surely live, he shall not die. None of his sins that he hath committed shall be mentioned unto him: he hath done that which is lawful and right; he shall surely live.

"Yet the children of thy people say, The way of the Lord is not equal: but as for them, their way is not equal. When the righteous turneth from his righteousness, and committeth iniquity, he shall even die thereby. But if the wicked turn from his wickedness, and do that which is lawful and right, he shall live thereby. Yet ye say, The way of the Lord is not equal. O ye house of Israel, I will judge you every one after his ways."

And it came to pass in the twelfth year of our captivity, in the tenth month, in the fifth day of the month, that one that had escaped out of Jerusalem came unto me, saying, "The city is smitten." Now the hand of the Lord was upon me in the evening, afore he that was escaped came; and had opened my mouth, until he came to me in the morning; and my mouth was opened, and I was no more dumb. Then the word of the Lord came unto me, saying,

"Son of man, they that inhabit those wastes of the land of Israel speak, saying, Abraham was one, and he inherited the land: but we are many; the land is given us for inheritance. Wherefore say unto them, Thus saith the Lord God; Ye eat with the blood. and lift up your eyes toward your idols, and shed blood: and shall ye possess the land? Ye stand upon your sword, ye work abomination, and ye defile every one his neighbour's wife: and shall ye possess the land? Say thou thus unto them, Thus saith the Lord God; As I live, surely they that are in the wastes shall fall by the sword, and him that is in the open field will I give to the beasts to be devoured, and they that be in the forts and in the caves shall die of the pestilence.

For I will lay the land most desolate, and the pomp of her strength shall cease; and the mountains of Israel shall be desolate, that none shall pass through. Then shall they know that I am the Lord, when I have laid the land most desolate because of all their abominations which they have committed.

"Also, thou son of man, the children of thy people still are talking against thee by the walls and in the doors of the houses, and speak one to another, every one to his brother, saying, Come, I pray you, and hear what is the word that cometh forth from the Lord. And they come unto thee as the people cometh, and they sit before thee as my people, and they hear thy words, but they will not do them: for with their mouth they shew much love, but their heart goeth after their covetousness. And, lo, thou art unto them as a very lovely song of one that hath a pleasant voice, and can play well on an instrument: for they hear thy words, but they do them not. And when this cometh to pass, (lo, it will come,) then shall they know that a prophet hath been among them."

And the word of the Lord came unto me, saying,

"Son of man, prophesy against the shepherds of Israel, prophesy, and say unto them, Thus saith the Lord God unto the shepherds; Woe be to the shepherds of Israel that do feed themselves! should not the shepherds feed the flocks? Ye eat the fat, and ye clothe you with the wool, ye kill them that are fed: but ye feed not the flock. The diseased have ye not strengthened, neither have ye healed that which was sick, neither have ye bound up that which was broken, neither have ye brought again that which was driven away, neither have ye sought that which was lost; but with force and with cruelty have ye ruled them. And they were scattered, because there is no shepherd: and they became meat to all the beasts of the field, when they were scattered. My sheep wandered through all the mountains, and upon every high hill: yea, my flock was scattered upon all the face of the earth, and none did search or seek after them.

"Therefore, ye shepherds, hear the word of the Lord; As I live, saith the Lord God, surely because my flock became a prey, and my flock became meat to every beast of the field, because there was no shepherd, neither did my shepherds search for my flock, but the shepherds fed themselves, and fed not my flock; therefore, O ye shepherds, hear the word of the Lord; thus saith the Lord God; Behold, I am against the shepherds; and I will require my flock at their hand, and cause them to cease from feeding the flock; neither shall the shepherds feed themselves any more; for I will deliver my flock from their mouth, that they may not be meat for them.

"For thus saith the Lord God; Behold, I, even I, will both search my sheep, and seek them out. As a shepherd seeketh out his flock in the day that he is among his sheep that are scattered; so will I seek out my sheep, and will deliver them out of all places where they have been scattered in the cloudy and dark day. And I will bring them out from the people, and gather them from the countries, and will bring them to their own land, and feed them upon the mountains of Israel by the rivers, and in all the inhabited places of the country. I will feed them in a good pasture, and upon the high mountains of Israel shall their fold be: there shall they lie in a good fold, and in a fat pasture shall they feed upon the mountains of Israel. I will feed my flock, and I will cause them to lie down, saith the Lord God. I will seek that which was lost, and bring again that which was driven away, and will bind up that which was broken, and will strengthen that which was sick: but I will destroy the fat and the strong; I will feed them with judgment.

"And as for you, O my flock, thus saith the Lord God; Behold, I judge between cattle and cattle, between the rams and the he goats. Seemeth it a small thing unto you to have eaten up the good pasture, but ye must tread down

with your feet the residue of your pastures? and
to have drunk of the deep waters, but ye must
foul the residue with your feet? And as for
my flock, they eat that which ye have trodden
with your feet; and they drink that which ye have
fouled with your feet. Therefore thus saith the
Lord God unto them; Behold, I, even I, will judge
between the fat cattle and between the lean
cattle. Because ye have thrust with side and with
shoulder, and pushed all the diseased with your
horns, till ye have scattered them abroad; therefore will I save my flock, and they shall no more
be a prey; and I will judge between cattle and
cattle. And I will set up one shepherd over
them, and he shall feed them, even my servant
David; he shall feed them, and he shall be
their shepherd. And I the Lord will be their
God, and my servant David a prince among
them; I the Lord have spoken it. And I will
make with them a covenant of peace, and will
cause the evil beasts to cease out of the land:
and they shall dwell safely in the wilderness,
and sleep in the woods. And I will make
them and the places round about my hill a
blessing; and I will cause the shower to come
down in his season; there shall be showers of
blessing. And the tree of the field shall yield
her fruit, and the earth shall yield her increase,
and they shall be safe in their land, and shall
know that I am the Lord, when I have broken

the bands of their yoke, and delivered them out of the hand of those that served themselves of them. And they shall no more be a prey to the heathen, neither shall the beast of the land devour them; but they shall dwell safely, and none shall make them afraid. And I will raise up for them a plant of renown, and they shall be no more consumed with hunger in the land, neither bear the shame of the heathen any more. Thus shall they know that I the Lord their God am with them, and that they, even the house of Israel, are my people, saith the Lord God.

"And ye my flock, the flock of my pasture, are men, and I am your God, saith the Lord God."

Moreover the word of the Lord came unto me, saying,

"Son of man, set thy face against mount Seir, and prophesy against it, and say unto it, Thus saith the Lord God; Behold, O mount Seir, I am against thee, and I will stretch out mine hand against thee, and I will make thee most desolate. I will lay thy cities waste, and thou shalt be desolate, and thou shalt know that I am the Lord.

"Because thou hast had a perpetual hatred, and hast shed the blood of the children of Israel by the force of the sword in the time of their calamity, in the time that their iniquity had an end: therefore, as I live, saith the Lord God, I will prepare thee unto blood, and blood shall pursue thee: sith thou hast not hated blood, even blood shall pursue thee. Thus will I make mount Seir most desolate, and cut off from it him that passeth out and him that returneth. And I will fill his mountains with his slain men: in thy hills, and in thy valleys, and in all thy rivers, shall they fall that are slain with the sword. I will make thee perpetual desolations, and thy cities shall not return: and ye shall know that I am the Lord.

"Because thou hast said, These two nations and these two countries shall be mine, and we will possess it; whereas the Lord was there: therefore, as I live, saith the Lord God, I will even do according to thine anger, and according to thine envy which thou hast used out of thy hatred against them: and I will make myself known among them, when I have judged thee. And thou shalt know that I am the Lord, and that I have heard all thy blasphemies which thou hast spoken against the mountains of Israel, saying, They are laid desolate, they are given us to consume. Thus with your mouth ye have boasted against me, and have multiplied your words against me: I have heard them. Thus saith the Lord God; When the whole earth rejoiceth, I will make thee desolate. As thou didst rejoice at the inheritance of the house of Israel, because it was desolate, so will I do unto thee: thou shalt be desolate, O mount Seir, and all Idumea, even all of it: and they shall know that I am the Lord.

"Also, thou son of man, prophesy unto the mountains of Israel, and say, Ye mountains of Israel, hear the word of the Lord: thus saith the Lord God; Because the enemy hath said against you, Aha, even the ancient high places are ours in possession: therefore prophesy and say, Thus saith the Lord God; Because they have made you desolate, and swallowed you up on every side, that ye might be a possession unto the residue of the heathen, and ye are taken up in the lips of talkers, and are an infamy of the people: therefore, ye mountains of Israel, hear the word of the Lord God; thus saith the Lord God to the mountains, and to the hills, to the rivers, and to the valleys, to the desolate wastes, and to the cities that are forsaken, which became a prey and derision to the residue of the heathen that are round about; therefore thus saith the Lord God ; surely in the fire of my jealousy have I spoken against the residue of the heathen, and against all Idumea, which have appointed my land into their possession with the joy of all their heart, with despiteful minds, to cast it out for a prey. Prophesy therefore concerning the land of Israel, and say unto the mountains, and to the hills, to the rivers, and to the valleys, Thus saith the Lord God; Behold, I have spoken in my jealousy and in my fury, because ye have borne the shame of the heathen: therefore thus saith the Lord God; I have lifted up mine hand; surely the heathen that are about you, they shall bear their shame. But ye, O mountains of Israel, ye shall shoot forth your branches, and yield your fruit to my people of Israel; for they are at hand to come.

"For, behold, I am for you, and I will turn unto you, and ye shall be tilled and sown: and I will multiply men upon you, all the house of Israel, even all of it: and the cities shall be inhabited, and the wastes shall be builded: and I will multiply upon you man and beast; and they shall increase and bring fruit: and I will settle you after your old estates, and will do better unto you than at your beginnings: and ye shall know that I am the Lord. Yea, I will cause men to walk upon you, even my people Israel; and they shall possess thee, and thou shalt be their inheritance, and thou shalt no more henceforth bereave them of men. Thus saith the Lord God; Because they say unto you, Thou land devourest up men, and hast bereaved thy nations; therefore thou shalt devour men no more, neither bereave thy nations any more, saith the Lord God. Neither will I cause men to hear in thee the shame of the heathen any more, neither shalt thou bear the reproach of the people any more, neither shalt thou cause thy nations to fall any more, saith the Lord God."

Moreover the word of the Lord came unto me, saying,

"Son of man, when the house of Israel dwelt in their own land, they defiled it by their own way and by their doings: their way was before me as the uncleanness of a removed woman. Wherefore I poured my fury upon them for the blood that they had shed upon the land, and for their idols wherewith they had polluted it: and I scattered them among the heathen, and they were dispersed through the countries: according to their way and according to their doings I judged them. And when they entered unto the heathen, whither they went, they profaned my holy name, when they said to them, These are the people of the Lord, and are gone forth out of his land. But I had pity for mine holy name, which the house of Israel had profaned among the heathen, whither they went.

"Therefore say unto the house of Israel, Thus saith the Lord God; I do not this for your sakes, O house of Israel, but for mine holy name's sake, which ye have profaned among the heathen, whither ye went. And I will sanctify my great name, which was profaned among the heathen, which ye have profaned in the midst of them; and the heathen shall know that I am the Lord, saith the Lord God, when I shall be sanctified in you before their eyes. For I will take you from among the heathen, and gather you out of all countries, and will bring you into your own land. Then will I sprinkle clean water upon you, and ye shall be clean: from all your filthiness, and from all your idols, will I cleanse you. A new heart also will I give you, and a new spirit will I put within you: and I will take away the stony heart out of your flesh, and I will give you an heart of flesh. And I will put my spirit within you, and cause you to walk in my statutes, and ye shall keep my judgments, and do them. And ye shall dwell in the land that I gave to your fathers; and ye shall be my people, and I will be your God.

"I will also save you from all your uncleannesses: and I will call for the corn, and will increase it, and lay no famine upon you. And I will multiply the fruit of the tree, and the increase of the field, that ye shall receive no more reproach of famine among the heathen. Then shall ye remember your own evil ways, and your doings that were not good, and shall loathe yourselves in your own sight for your iniquities and for your abominations. Not for your sakes do I this, saith the Lord God, be it known unto you: be ashamed and confounded for your own ways, O house of Israel.

"Thus saith the Lord God; In the day that I shall have cleansed you from all your iniquities I will also cause you to dwell in the cities, and the wastes shall be builded. And the desolate land shall be tilled, whereas it lay desolate in the sight of all that passed by. And they shall say, This land that was desolate is become like the garden of Eden; and the waste and desolate and ruined cities are become fenced, and are inhabited. Then the heathen that are left round about you shall know that I the Lord build the ruined places, and plant that that was desolate: I the Lord have spoken it, and I will do it.

"Thus saith the Lord God; I will yet for this be enquired of by the house of Israel, to do it for them; I will increase them with men like a flock. As the holy flock, as the flock of Jerusalem in her solemn feasts; so shall the waste cities be filled with flocks of men: and they shall know that I am the Lord."

The hand of the Lord was upon me, and carried me out in the spirit of the Lord, and set me down in the midst of the valley which was full of bones, and caused me to pass by them round about: and, behold, there were very many in the open valley; and, lo, they were very dry. And he said unto me "Son of man, can these bones live?" And I answered, "O Lord God, thou knowest."

Again he said unto me, "Prophesy upon these bones, and say unto them, O ye dry bones, hear the word of the Lord. Thus saith the Lord God unto these bones; Behold, I will cause breath to enter into you, and ye shall live: and I will lay sinews upon you, and will bring up flesh upon you, and cover you with skin, and put breath in you, and ye shall live; and ye shall know that I am the Lord."

So I prophesied as I was commanded: and as I prophesied, there was a noise, and behold a shaking, and the bones came together, bone to his bone. And when I beheld, lo, the sinews and the flesh came up upon them, and the skin covered them above: but there was no breath in them.

Then said he unto me, "Prophesy unto the wind, prophesy, son of man, and say to the wind, Thus saith the Lord God; Come from the four winds, O breath, and breathe upon these slain, that they may live." So I prophesied as he commanded me, and the breath came into them, and they lived, and stood up upon their feet, an exceeding great army.

Then he said unto me, "Son of man, these bones are the whole house of Israel: behold, they say, Our bones are dried, and our hope is lost: we are cut off for our parts. Therefore prophesy and say unto them, Thus saith the Lord God; Behold, O my people, I will open your graves, and cause you to come up out of your graves, and bring you into the land of Israel. And ye shall know that I am the Lord, when I have opened your graves, O my people, and brought you up out of your graves, and shall put my spirit in you, and ye shall live, and I shall place you in your own land: then shall ye know that I the Lord have spoken it, and performed it, saith the Lord."

The word of the Lord came again unto me, saying,

"Moreover, thou son of man, take thee one stick, and write upon it, For Judah, and for the children of Israel his companions: then take another stick, and write upon it, For Joseph, the stick of Ephraim, and for all the house of Israel his companions: and join them one to another into one stick; and they shall become one in thine hand. And when the children of thy people shall speak unto thee, saying, Wilt thou not shew us what thou meanest by these? say unto them, Thus saith the Lord God; Behold, I will take the stick of Joseph, which is in the hand of Ephraim, and the tribes of Israel his fellows, and will put them with him, even with the stick of Judah, and make them one stick, and they shall be one in mine hand. And the sticks whereon thou writest shall be in thine hand before their eyes.

"And say unto them, Thus saith the Lord God; Behold, I will take the children of Israel from among the heathen, whither they be gone, and will gather them on every side, and bring them into their own land: and I will make them one nation in the land upon the mountains of Israel; and one king shall be king to them all: and they shall be no more two nations, neither shall they be divided into two kingdoms any more at all: neither shall they defile themselves any more with their idols, nor with their detestable things, nor with any of their transgressions: but I will save them out of all their dwellingplaces, wherein they have sinned, and will cleanse them: so shall they be my people, and I will be their God. And David my servant shall be king over them; and they all shall have one shepherd: they shall also walk in my judgments, and observe my statutes, and do them. And they shall dwell in the land that I have given unto Jacob my servant, wherein your fathers have dwelt; and they shall dwell therein, even they, and their children, and their children's children for ever: and my servant David shall be their prince for ever. Moreover I will make a covenant of peace with them; it shall be an everlasting covenant with them: and I will place them, and multiply them, and will set my sanctuary in the midst of them for evermore. My tabernacle also shall be with them: yea, I will be their God, and they shall be my people. And the heathen shall know that I the Lord do sanctify Israel, when my sanctuary shall be in the midst of them for evermore."

And the word of the Lord came unto me, saying,

"Son of man, set thy face against Gog, the land of Magog, the chief prince of Meshech and Tubal, and prophesy against him, and say, Thus saith the Lord God; Behold, I am against thee, O Gog, the chief prince of Meshech and Tubal: and I will turn thee back, and put hooks into thy jaws, and I will bring thee forth, and all thine army, horses and horsemen, all of them clothed with all sorts of armour, even a great company with bucklers and shields, all of them handling swords: Persia, Ethiopia, and Libya with them; all of them with shield and helmet: Gomer, and all his bands; the house of Togarmah of the north quarters, and all his bands: and many people with thee.

"Be thou prepared, and prepare for thyself, thou, and all thy company that are assembled unto thee, and be thou a guard unto them. After many days thou shalt be visited: in the latter years thou shalt come into the land that is brought back from the sword, and is gathered

out of many people, against the mountains of
Israel, which have been always waste: but it is
brought forth out of the nations, and they shall
dwell safely all of them. Thou shalt ascend
and come like a storm, thou shalt be like a
cloud to cover the land, thou, and all thy bands,
and many people with thee.

"Thus saith the Lord God; It shall also come
to pass, that at the same time shall things come
into thy mind, and thou shalt think an evil
thought: and thou shalt say, I will go up to
the land of unwalled villages; I will go to them
that are at rest, that dwell safely, all of them
dwelling without walls, and having neither bars
nor gates, to take a spoil, and to take a prey;
to turn thine hand upon the desolate places
that are now inhabited, and upon the people
that are gathered out of the nations, which have
gotten cattle and goods, that dwell in the midst
of the land. Sheba, and Dedan, and the merchants of Tarshish, with all the young lions
thereof, shall say unto thee, Art thou come to
take a spoil? hast thou gathered thy company
to take a prey? to carry away silver and gold,
to take away cattle and goods, to take a great
spoil? Therefore, son of man, prophesy and
say unto Gog, Thus saith the Lord God; In
that day when my people of Israel dwelleth
safely, shalt thou not know it? And thou shalt
come from thy place out of the north parts,

thou, and many people with thee, all of them riding upon horses, a great company, and a mighty army: and thou shalt come up against my people of Israel, as a cloud to cover the land; it shall be in the latter days, and I will bring thee against my land, that the heathen may know me, when I shall be sanctified in thee, O Gog, before their eyes.

"Thus saith the Lord God; Art thou he of whom I have spoken in old time by my servants the prophets of Israel, which prophesied in those days many years that I would bring thee against them? And it shall come to pass at the same time when Gog shall come against the land of Israel, saith the Lord God, that my fury shall come up in my face. For in my jealousy and in the fire of my wrath have I spoken, Surely in that day there shall be a great shaking in the land of Israel; so that the fishes of the sea, and the fowls of the heaven, and the beasts of the field, and all creeping things that creep upon the earth, and all the men that are upon the face of the earth, shall shake at my presence, and the mountains shall be thrown down, and the steep places shall fall, and every wall shall fall to the ground. And I will call for a sword against him throughout all my mountains, saith the Lord God: every man's sword shall be against his brother. And I will plead against him with pestilence and with blood; and I will rain upon him, and upon his bands, and upon the many people that are with him, an overflowing rain, and great hailstones, fire, and brimstone. Thus will I magnify myself, and sanctify myself; and I will be known in the eyes of many nations, and they shall know that I am the Lord.

"Therefore, thou son of man, prophesy against Gog, and say, Thus saith the Lord God; Behold, I am against thee, O Gog, the chief prince of Meshech and Tubal: and I will turn thee back, and leave but the sixth part of thee, and will cause thee to come up from the north parts, and will bring thee upon the mountains of Israel: and I will smite thy bow out of thy left hand, and will cause thine arrows to fall out of thy right hand. Thou shalt fall upon the mountains of Israel, thou, and all thy bands, and the people that is with thee: I will give thee unto the ravenous birds of every sort, and to the beasts of the field to be devoured. Thou shalt fall upon the open field: for I have spoken it, saith the Lord God. And I will send a fire on Magog, and among them that dwell carelessly in the isles: and they shall know that I am the Lord. So will I make my holy name known in the midst of my people Israel; and I will not let them pollute my holy name any more: and the heathen shall know that I am the Lord, the Holy One in Israel.

"Behold, it is come, and it is done, saith the Lord God; this is the day whereof I have spoken. And they that dwell in the cities of Israel shall go forth, and shall set on fire and burn the weapons, both the shields and the bucklers, the bows and the arrows, and the handstaves, and the spears, and they shall burn them with fire seven years: so that they shall take no wood out of the field, neither cut down any out of the forests; for they shall burn the weapons with fire: and they shall spoil those that spoiled them, and rob those that robbed them, saith the Lord God.

"And it shall come to pass in that day, that I will give unto Gog a place there of graves in Israel, the valley of the passengers on the east of the sea: and it shall stop the noses of the passengers: and there shall they bury Gog and all his multitude: and they shall call it The valley of Hamon-gog. And seven months shall the house of Israel be burying of them, that they may cleanse the land. Yea, all the people of the land shall bury them; and it shall be to them a renown the day that I shall be glorified, saith the Lord God. And they shall sever out men of continual employment, passing through the land to bury with the passengers those that remain upon the face of the earth, to cleanse it: after the end of seven months shall they search. And the passengers that pass through the land, when any seeth a man's bone, then shall he set up a sign by it, till the buriers have buried it in the valley of Hamon-gog. And also the name of the city shall be Hamonah. Thus shall they cleanse the land.

"And, thou son of man, thus saith the Lord God; Speak unto every feathered fowl, and to every beast of the field, Assemble yourselves, and come; gather yourselves on every side to my sacrifice that I do sacrifice for you, even a great sacrifice upon the mountains of Israel, that ye may eat flesh, and drink blood. Ye shall eat the flesh of the mighty, and drink the blood of the princes of the earth, of rams, of lambs, and of goats, of bullocks, all of them fatlings of Bashan. And ye shall eat fat till ye be full, and drink blood till ye be drunken, of my sacrifice which I have sacrificed for you. Thus ye shall be filled at my table with horses and chariots, with mighty men, and with all men of war, saith the Lord God.

"And I will set my glory among the heathen, and all the heathen shall see my judgment that I have executed, and my hand that I have laid upon them. So the house of Israel shall know that I am the Lord their God from that day and forward. And the heathen shall know that the house of Israel went into captivity for their iniquity: because they trespassed against me, therefore hid I my face from them, and gave them into the hand of their enemies: so fell they all by the sword. According to their uncleanness and according to their transgressions have I done unto them, and hid my face from them. Therefore thus saith the Lord God; Now will I bring again the captivity of Jacob, and have mercy upon the whole house of Israel, and will be jealous for my holy name; after that they have borne their shame, and all their trespasses whereby they have trespassed against me, when they dwelt safely in their land, and none made them afraid. When I have brought them again from the people, and gathered them out of their enemies' lands, and am sanctified in them in the sight of many nations; then shall they know that I am the Lord their God, which caused them to be led into captivity among the heathen: but I have gathered them unto their own land, and have left none of them any more there. Neither will I hide my face any more from them: for I have poured out my spirit upon the house of Israel, saith the Lord God."

IN THE five and twentieth year of our captivity, in the beginning of the year, in the tenth day of the month, in the fourteenth year after that the city was smitten, in the selfsame day the hand of the Lord was upon me, and brought me thither. In the visions of God brought he me into the land of Israel, and set me upon a very high mountain, by which was as the frame of a city on the south. And he brought me thither, and, behold, there was a man, whose appearance was like the appearance of brass, with a line of flax in his hand, and a measuring reed; and he stood in the gate. And the man said unto me, "Son of man, behold with thine eyes, and hear with thine ears, and set thine heart upon all that I shall shew thee; for to the intent that I might shew them unto thee art thou brought hither: declare all that thou seest to the house of Israel."

And behold a wall on the outside of the house round about, and in the man's hand a measuring reed of six cubits long by the cubit and an hand breadth: so he measured the breadth of the building, one reed; and the height, one reed.

Then came he unto the gate which looketh toward the east, and went up the stairs thereof, and measured the threshold of the gate, which was one reed broad; and the other threshold of the gate, which was one reed broad. And every little chamber was one reed long, and one reed broad; and between the little chambers were five cubits; and the threshold of the gate by the porch of the gate within was one reed. He measured also the porch of the gate within, one reed.

Then measured he the porch of the gate,

eight cubits; and the posts thereof, two cubits; and the porch of the gate was inward. And the little chambers of the gate eastward were three on this side, and three on that side; they three were of one measure: and the posts had one measure on this side and on that side. And he measured the breadth of the entry of the gate, ten cubits; and the length of the gate, thirteen cubits. The space also before the little chambers was one cubit on this side, and the space was one cubit on that side: and the little chambers were six cubits on this side, and six cubits on that side.

He measured then the gate from the roof of one little chamber to the roof of another: the breadth was five and twenty cubits, door against door. He made also posts of threescore cubits, even unto the post of the court round about the gate. And from the face of the gate of the entrance unto the face of the porch of the inner gate were fifty cubits. And there were narrow windows to the little chambers, and to their posts within the gate round about, and likewise to the arches: and windows were round about inward: and upon each post were palm trees.

Then brought he me into the outward court, and, lo, there were chambers, and a pavement made for the court round about: thirty chambers were upon the pavement. And the pavement by the side of the gates over against the length of the gates was the lower pavement.

Then he measured the breadth from the forefront of the lower gate unto the forefront of the inner court without, an hundred cubits eastward and northward. And the gate of the outward court that looked toward the north, he measured the length thereof, and the breadth thereof. And the little chambers thereof were three on this side and three on that side; and the posts thereof and the arches thereof were after the measure of the first gate: the length thereof was fifty cubits, and the breadth five and twenty cubits. And their windows, and their arches, and their palm trees, were after the measure of the gate that looketh toward the east; and they went up unto it by seven steps; and the arches thereof were before them. And the gate of the inner court was over against the gate toward the north, and toward the east; and he measured from gate to gate an hundred cubits.

After that he brought me toward the south, and behold a gate toward the south: and he measured the posts thereof and the arches thereof according to these measures. And there were windows in it and in the arches thereof round about, like those windows: the length was fifty cubits, and the breadth five and twenty cubits. And there were seven steps to go up to it, and the arches thereof were before them: and it had palm trees, one on this side, and another on that side, upon the posts thereof. And there was a gate in the inner court toward the south: and he measured from gate to gate toward the south an hundred cubits.

And he brought me to the inner court by the south gate: and he measured the south gate according to these measures; and the little chambers thereof, and the posts thereof, and the arches thereof, according to these measures: and there were windows in it and in the arches thereof round about: it was fifty cubits long, and five and twenty cubits broad. And the arches round about were five and twenty cubits long, and five cubits broad. And the arches thereof were toward the utter court; and palm trees were upon the posts thereof: and the going up to it had eight steps.

And he brought me into the inner court toward the east: and he measured the gate according to these measures. And the little chambers thereof, and the posts thereof, and the arches thereof, were according to these measures: and there were windows therein and in the arches thereof round about: it was fifty cubits long, and five and twenty cubits broad. And the arches thereof were toward the outward court; and palm trees were upon the posts thereof, on this side, and on that side: and the going up to it had eight steps.

And he brought me to the north gate, and measured it according to these measures; the little chambers thereof, the posts thereof, and the arches thereof, and the windows to it round about: the length was fifty cubits, and the breadth five and twenty cubits. And the posts thereof were toward the utter court; and palm trees were upon the posts thereof, on this side, and on that side: and the going up to it had eight steps. And the chambers and the entries thereof were by the posts of the gates, where they washed the burnt offering.

And in the porch of the gate were two tables on this side, and two tables on that side, to slay thereon the burnt offering and the sin offering and the trespass offering. And at the side without, as one goeth up to the entry of the north gate, were two tables; and on the other side, which was at the porch of the gate, were two tables. Four tables were on this side, and four tables on that side, by the side of the gate; eight tables, whereupon they slew their sacrifices. And the four tables were of hewn stone for the burnt offering, of a cubit and an half long, and a cubit and an half broad, and one cubit high: whereupon also they laid the instruments wherewith they slew the burnt offering and the sacrifice. And within were hooks, an hand broad, fastened round about: and upon the tables was the flesh of the offering.

And without the inner gate were the chambers of the singers in the inner court, which was at the side of the north gate; and their prospect was toward the south: one at the side of the east gate having the prospect toward the north. And he said unto me, "This chamber, whose prospect is toward the south, is for the priests, the keepers of the charge of the house. And the chamber whose prospect is toward the north is for the priests, the keepers of the charge of the altar: these are the sons of Zadok among the sons of Levi, which come near to the Lord to minister unto him."

So he measured the court, an hundred cubits long, and an hundred cubits broad, foursquare; and the altar that was before the house. And he brought me to the porch of the house, and measured each post of the porch, five cubits on this side, and five cubits on that side: and the breadth of the gate was three cubits on this side, and three cubits on that side. The length of the porch was twenty cubits, and the breadth eleven cubits; and he brought me by the steps whereby they went up to it: and there were pillars by the posts, one on this side, and another on that side.

Afterward he brought me to the temple, and measured the posts, six cubits broad on the one side, and six cubits broad on the other side, which was the breadth of the tabernacle. And the breadth of the door was ten cubits; and the sides of the door were five cubits on the one side, and five cubits on the other side: and he measured the length thereof, forty cubits: and the breadth, twenty cubits. Then went he inward, and measured the post of the door, two cubits; and the door, six cubits; and the breadth of the door, seven cubits. So he measured the length thereof, twenty cubits; and the breadth, twenty cubits, before the temple: and he said unto me, "This is the most holy place."

After he measured the wall of the house, six cubits; and the breadth of every side chamber, four cubits, round about the house on every side. And the side chambers were three, one over another, and thirty in order; and they entered into the wall which was of the house for the side chambers round about, that they might have hold, but they had not hold in the wall of the house. And there was an enlarging, and a winding about still upward to the side chambers: for the winding about of the house went still upward round about the house: therefore the breadth of the house was still upward, and so increased from the lowest chamber to the highest by the midst. I saw also the height of the house round about: the foundations of the side chambers were a full reed of six great cubits. The thickness of the wall, which was for the side chamber without, was five cubits: and that which was left was the place of the side chambers that were within. And between the chambers was the wideness of twenty cubits round about the house on every side. And the doors of the side chambers were toward the place that was left, one door toward the north, and another door toward the south: and the breadth of the place that was left was five cubits round about.

Now the building that was before the separate place at the end toward the west was seventy cubits broad; and the wall of the building was five cubits thick round about, and the length thereof ninety cubits. So he measured the house, an hundred cubits long; and the separate place, and the building, with the walls thereof, an hundred cubits long; also the breadth of the face of the house, and of the separate place toward the east, an hundred cubits.

And he measured the length of the building over against the separate place which was behind it, and the galleries thereof on the one side and on the other side, an hundred cubits, with the inner temple, and the porches of the court; the door posts, and the narrow windows, and the galleries round about on their three stories, over against the door, cieled with wood round about, and from the ground up to the windows, and the windows were covered; to that above the door, even unto the inner house, and without, and by all the wall round about within and without, by measure. And it was made with cherubims and palm trees, so that a palm tree was between a cherub and a cherub; and every cherub had two faces; so that the face of a man was toward the palm tree on the one side, and the face of a young lion toward the palm tree on the other side: it was made through all the house round about. From the ground unto above the door were cherubims and palm trees made, and on the wall of the temple. The posts of the temple were squared, and the face of the sanctuary; the appearance of the one as the appearance of the other.

The altar of wood was three cubits high, and the length thereof two cubits; and the corners thereof, and the length thereof, and the walls thereof, were of wood: and he said unto me, "This is the table that is before the Lord."

And the temple and the sanctuary had two doors. And the doors had two leaves apiece, two turning leaves; two leaves for the one door, and two leaves for the other door. And there were made on them, on the doors of the temple, cherubims and palm trees, like as were made upon the walls; and there were thick planks upon the face of the porch without. And there were narrow windows and palm trees on the one side and on the other side, on the sides of the porch, and upon the side chambers of the house, and thick planks.

Then he brought me forth into the utter court, the way toward the north: and he brought me into the chamber that was over against the separate place, and which was before the building toward the north. Before the length of an hundred cubits was the north door, and the breadth was fifty cubits. Over against the twenty cubits which were for the inner court, and over against the pavement which was for the utter court, was gallery against gallery in three stories. And before the chambers was a walk of ten cubits breadth inward, a way of one cubit; and their doors toward the north. Now the upper chambers were shorter: for the galleries were higher than these, than the lower, and than the middlemost of the building. For they were in three stories, but had not pillars as the pillars of the courts: therefore the building was straitened more than the lowest and the middlemost from the ground.

And the wall that was without over against the chambers, toward the utter court on the forepart of the chambers, the length thereof was fifty cubits. For the length of the chambers that were in the utter court was fifty cubits: and, lo, before the temple were an hundred cubits. And from under these chambers was the entry on the east side, as one goeth into them from the utter court. The chambers were in the thickness of the wall of the court toward the east, over against the separate place, and over against the building. And the way before them was like the appearance of the chambers which were toward the north, as long as they, and as broad as they: and all their goings out were both according to their fashions, and according to their doors. And according to the doors of the chambers that were toward the south was a door in the head of the way, even the way directly before the wall toward the east, as one entereth into them.

Then said he unto me, "The north chambers and the south chambers, which are before the separate place, they be holy chambers, where the priests that approach unto the Lord shall eat the most holy things: there shall they lay the most holy things, and the meat offering, and the sin offering, and the trespass offering; for the place is holy. When the priests enter therein, then shall they not go out of the holy place into the utter court, but there they shall lay their garments wherein they minister; for they are holy; and shall put on other garments, and shall approach to those things which are for the people."

Now when he had made an end of measuring the inner house, he brought me forth toward the gate whose prospect is toward the east, and measured it round about. He measured the east side with the measuring reed, five hundred reeds, with the measuring reed round about. He measured the north side, five hundred reeds, with the measuring reed round about. He measured the south side, five hundred reeds, with the measuring reed. He turned about to the west side, and measured five hundred reeds with the measuring reed. He measured it by the four sides: it had a wall round about, five hundred reeds long, and five hundred broad, to make a separation between the sanctuary and the profane place.

Afterward he brought me to the gate, even the gate that looketh toward the east: and, behold, the glory of the God of Israel came from the way of the east: and his voice was like a noise of many waters: and the earth shined with his glory. And it was according to the appearance of the vision which I saw, even according to the vision that I saw when I came to destroy the city: and the visions were like the vision that I saw by the river Chebar; and I fell upon my face. And the glory of the Lord came into the house by the way of the gate whose prospect is toward the east.

So the spirit took me up, and brought me into the inner court; and, behold, the glory of the Lord filled the house. And I heard him speaking unto me out of the house; and the man stood by me. And he said unto me, "Son of man, the place of my throne, and the place of the soles of my feet, where I will dwell in the midst of the children of Israel for ever, and my holy name, shall the house of Israel no more defile, neither they, nor their kings, by their whoredom, nor by the carcases of their kings in their high places. In their setting of their threshold by my thresholds, and their post by my posts, and the wall between me and them, they have even defiled my holy name by their abominations that they have committed: wherefore I have consumed them in mine anger. Now let them put away their whoredom, and the carcases of their kings, far from me, and I will dwell in the midst of them for ever. Thou son of man, shew the house to the house of Israel, that they may be ashamed of their iniquities: and let them measure the pattern. And if they be ashamed of all that they have done, shew them the form of the house, and the fashion thereof, and the goings out thereof, and the comings in thereof, and all the forms thereof, and all the ordinances thereof, and all the forms thereof, and all the laws thereof: and write it in their sight, that they may keep the whole form thereof, and all the ordinances thereof, and do them.

"This is the law of the house; Upon the top of the mountain the whole limit thereof round about shall be most holy. Behold, this is the law of the house.

"And these are the measures of the altar after the cubits: The cubit is a cubit and an hand breadth; even the bottom shall be a cubit, and the breadth a cubit, and the border thereof by the edge thereof round about shall be a span: and this shall be the higher place of the altar. And from the bottom upon the ground even to the lower settle shall be two cubits, and the breadth one cubit; and from the lesser settle even to the greater settle shall be four cubits, and the breadth one cubit. So the altar shall be four cubits; and from the altar and upward shall be four horns. And the altar shall be twelve cubits long, twelve broad, square in the four squares thereof. And the settle shall be fourteen cubits long and fourteen broad in the four squares thereof; and the border about it shall be half a cubit; and the bottom thereof shall be a cubit about; and his stairs shall look toward the east."

And he said unto me, "Son of man, thus saith the Lord God; These are the ordinances of the altar in the day when they shall make it, to offer burnt offerings thereon, and to sprinkle blood thereon.

"And thou shalt give to the priests the Levites that be of the seed of Zadok, which approach unto me, to minister unto me, saith the Lord

God, a young bullock for a sin offering. And thou shalt take of the blood thereof, and put it on the four horns of it, and on the four corners of the settle, and upon the border round about: thus shalt thou cleanse and purge it. Thou shalt take the bullock also of the sin offering, and he shall burn it in the appointed place of the house, without the sanctuary. And on the second day thou shalt offer a kid of the goats without blemish for a sin offering; and they shall cleanse the altar, as they did cleanse it with the bullock. When thou hast made an end of cleansing it, thou shalt offer a young bullock without blemish, and a ram out of the flock without blemish. And thou shalt offer them before the Lord, and the priests shall cast salt upon them, and they shall offer them up for a burnt offering unto the Lord. Seven days shalt thou prepare every day a goat for a sin offering: they shall also prepare a young bullock, and a ram out of the flock, without blemish. Seven days shall they purge the altar and purify it; and they shall consecrate themselves. And when these days are expired, it shall be, that upon the eighth day, and so forward, the priests shall make your burnt offerings upon the altar, and your peace offerings; and I will accept you, saith the Lord God."

Then he brought me back the way of the gate of the outward sanctuary which looketh toward the east: and it was shut. Then said the Lord unto me; "This gate shall be shut, it shall not be opened, and no man shall enter in by it; because the Lord, the God of Israel, hath entered in by it, therefore it shall be shut. It is for the prince; the prince, he shall sit in it to eat bread before the Lord; he shall enter by the way of the porch of that gate, and shall go out by the way of the same."

Then brought he me the way of the north gate before the house: and I looked, and, behold, the glory of the Lord filled the house of the Lord: and I fell upon my face. And the Lord said unto me, "Son of man, mark well, and behold with thine eyes, and hear with thine ears all that I say unto thee concerning all the ordinances of the house of the Lord, and all the laws thereof; and mark well the entering in of the house, with every going forth of the sanctuary.

"And thou shalt say to the rebellious, even to the house of Israel, Thus saith the Lord God; O ye house of Israel, let it suffice you of all your abominations, in that ye have brought into my sanctuary strangers, uncircumcised in heart, and uncircumcised in flesh, to be in my sanctuary, to pollute it, even my house, when ye offer my bread, the fat and the blood, and they have broken my covenant because of all your abominations. And ye have not kept the charge of mine holy things: but ye have set keepers of my charge in my sanctuary for yourselves. Thus saith the Lord God; No stranger, uncircumcised in heart, nor uncircumcised in flesh, shall enter into my sanctuary, of any stranger that is among the children of Israel.

"And the Levites that are gone away far from me, when Israel went astray, which went astray away from me after their idols; they shall even bear their iniquity. Yet they shall be ministers in my sanctuary, having charge at the gates of the house, and ministering to the house: they shall slay the burnt offering and the sacrifice for the people, and they shall stand before them to minister unto them. Because they ministered unto them before their idols, and caused the house of Israel to fall into iniquity; therefore have I lifted up mine hand against them, saith the Lord God, and they shall bear their iniquity. And they shall not come near unto me, to do the office of a priest unto me, nor to come near to any of my holy things, in the most holy place: but they shall bear their shame, and their abominations which they have committed. But I will make them keepers of the charge of the house, for all the service thereof, and for all that shall be done therein. But the priests the Levites, the sons of Zadok, that kept the charge of my sanctuary when the children of Israel went astray from me, they shall come near to me to minister unto me, and they shall stand before me to offer unto me the fat and the blood, saith the Lord God: they shall enter into my sanctuary, and they shall come near to my table, to minister unto me, and they shall keep my charge.

"And it shall come to pass, that when they enter in at the gates of the inner court, they shall be clothed with linen garments; and no wool shall come upon them, whiles they minister in the gates of the inner court, and within. They shall have linen bonnets upon their heads, and shall have linen breeches upon their loins; they shall not gird themselves with any thing that causeth sweat. And when they go forth into the utter court, even into the utter court to the people, they shall put off their garments wherein they ministered, and lay them in the holy chambers, and they shall put on other garments; and they shall not sanctify the people with their garments. Neither shall they shave their heads, nor suffer their locks to grow long; they shall only poll their heads. Neither shall any priest drink wine, when they enter into the inner court. Neither shall they take for their wives a widow, nor her that is put away: but they shall take maidens of the seed of the house of Israel, or a widow that had a priest before. And they shall teach my people the difference between the holy and profane, and cause them to discern between the unclean and the clean. And in controversy they shall stand in judgment; and they shall judge it according to my judgments: and they shall keep my laws and my statutes in all mine assemblies; and they shall hallow my sabbaths. And they shall come at no dead person to defile themselves: but for father, or for mother, or for son, or for daughter, for brother, or for sister that hath had no husband, they may defile themselves. And after he is cleansed, they shall reckon unto him seven days. And in the day that he goeth into the sanctuary, unto the inner court, to minister in the sanctuary, he shall offer his sin offering, saith the Lord God. And it shall be unto them for an inheritance: I am their inheritance: and ye shall give them no possession in Israel: I am their possession. They shall eat the meat offering, and the sin offering, and the trespass offering; and every dedicated thing in Israel shall be theirs. And the first of all the firstfruits of all things, and every oblation of all, of every sort of your oblations, shall be the priest's: ye shall also give unto the priest the first of your dough, that he may cause the blessing to rest in thine house. The priests shall not eat of any thing that is dead of itself, or torn, whether it be fowl or beast.

" Moreover, when ye shall divide by lot the land for inheritance, ye shall offer an oblation unto the Lord, an holy portion of the land: the length shall be the length of five and twenty thousand reeds, and the breadth shall be ten thousand. This shall be holy in all the borders thereof round about. Of this there shall be for the sanctuary five hundred in length, with five hundred in breadth, square round about; and fifty cubits round about for the suburbs thereof. And of this measure shalt thou measure the length of five and twenty thousand, and the breadth of ten thousand: and in it shall be the sanctuary and the most holy place. The holy portion of the land shall be for the priests the ministers of the sanctuary, which shall come near to minister unto the Lord: and it shall be a place for their houses, and an holy place for the sanctuary. And the five and twenty thousand of length, and the ten thousand of breadth, shall also the Levites, the ministers of the house, have for themselves, for a possession for twenty chambers.

"And ye shall appoint the possession of the city five thousand broad, and five and twenty thousand long, over against the oblation of the holy portion: it shall be for the whole house of Israel.

"And a portion shall be for the prince on the one side and on the other side of the oblation of the holy portion, and of the possession of the city, before the oblation of the holy portion, and before the possession of the city, from the west side westward, and from the east side eastward: and the length shall be over against one of the portions, from the west border unto the east border. In the land shall be his possession in Israel: and my princes shall no more oppress my people; and the rest of the land shall they give to the house of Israel according to their tribes.

"Thus saith the Lord God; Let it suffice you, O princes of Israel: remove violence and spoil, and execute judgment and justice, take away your exactions from my people, saith the Lord God. Ye shall have just balances, and a just ephah, and a just bath. The ephah and the bath shall be of one measure, that the bath may contain the tenth part of an homer, and the ephah the tenth part of an homer: the measure thereof shall be after the homer. And the shekel shall be twenty gerahs: twenty shekels, five and twenty shekels, fifteen shekels, shall be your maneh.

"This is the oblation that ye shall offer, the sixth part of an ephah of an homer of wheat; and ye shall give the sixth part of an ephah of an homer of barley: concerning the ordinance of oil, the bath of oil, ye shall offer the tenth part of a bath out of the cor, which is an homer of ten baths; for ten baths are an homer: and one lamb out of the flock, out of two hundred, out of the fat pastures of Israel; for a meat offering, and for a burnt offering, and for peace offerings, to make reconciliation for them, saith the Lord God. All the people of the land shall give this oblation for the prince in Israel. And it shall be the prince's part to give burnt offerings, and meat offerings, and drink offerings, in the feasts, and in the new moons, and in the sabbaths, in all solemnities of the house of Israel: he shall prepare the sin offering, and the meat offering, and the burnt offering, and the peace offerings, to make reconciliation for the house of Israel.

"Thus saith the Lord God; In the first month, in the first day of the month, thou shalt take a young bullock without blemish, and cleanse the sanctuary: and the priest shall take of the blood of the sin offering, and put it upon the posts of the house, and upon the four corners of the settle of the altar, and upon the posts of the gate of the inner court. And so thou shalt do the seventh day of the month for every one that erreth, and for him that is simple: so shall ye reconcile the house. In the first month, in the fourteenth day of the month, ye shall have the passover, a feast of seven days; unleavened bread shall be eaten. And upon that day shall the prince prepare for himself and for all the people of the land a bullock for a sin offering. And seven days of the feast he shall prepare a burnt offering to the Lord, seven bullocks and seven rams without blemish daily the seven days; and a kid of the goats daily for a sin offering. And he shall prepare a meat offering of an ephah for a bullock, and an ephah for a ram, and an hin of oil for an ephah. In the seventh month, in the fifteenth day of the month, shall he do the like in the feast of the seven days, according to the sin offering, according to the burnt offering, and according to the meat offering, and according to the oil.

"Thus saith the Lord God; The gate of the inner court that looketh toward the east shall be shut the six working days; but on the sabbath it shall be opened, and in the day of the new moon it shall be opened. And the prince shall enter by the way of the porch of that gate without, and shall stand by the post of the gate, and the priests shall prepare his burnt offering and his peace offerings, and he shall worship at the threshold of the gate: then he shall go forth; but the gate shall not be shut until the evening. Likewise the people of the land shall worship at the door of this gate before the Lord in the sabbaths and in the new moons. And the burnt offering that the prince shall offer unto the Lord in the sabbath day shall be six lambs without blemish, and a ram without blemish. And the meat offering shall be an ephah for a ram, and the meat offering for the lambs as he shall be able to give, and an hin of oil to an ephah. And in the day of the new moon it shall be a young bullock without blemish, and six lambs, and a ram: they shall be without blemish. And he shall prepare a meat offering, an ephah for a bullock, and an ephah for a ram, and for the lambs according as his hand shall attain unto, and an hin of oil to an ephah. And when the prince shall enter, he shall go in by the way of the porch of that gate, and he shall go forth by the way thereof. But when the people of the land shall come before the Lord in the solemn feasts, he that entereth in by the way of the north gate to worship shall go out by the way of the south gate; and he that entereth by the way of the south gate shall go forth by the way of the north gate: he shall not return by the way of the gate whereby he came in, but shall go forth over against it. And the prince in the midst of them, when they go in, shall go in; and when they go forth, shall go forth. And in the feasts and in the solemnities the meat offering shall be an ephah to a bullock, and an ephah to a ram, and to the lambs as he is able to give, and an hin of oil to an ephah. Now when the prince shall prepare a voluntary burnt offering or peace offerings voluntarily unto the Lord, one shall then open him the gate that looketh toward the east, and he shall prepare his burnt offering and his peace offerings, as he did on the sabbath day: then he shall go forth; and after his going forth one shall shut the gate.

"Thou shalt daily prepare a burnt offering unto the Lord of a lamb of the first year without blemish: thou shalt prepare it every morning. And thou shalt prepare a meat offering for it every morning, the sixth part of an ephah, and the third part of an hin of oil, to temper with the fine flour; a meat offering continually by a perpetual ordinance unto the Lord. Thus shall they prepare the lamb, and the meat offering, and the oil, every morning for a continual burnt offering.

"Thus saith the Lord God; If the prince give a gift unto any of his sons, the inheritance thereof shall be his sons'; it shall be their possession by inheritance. But if he give a gift of his inheritance to one of his servants, then it shall be his to the year of liberty; after it shall return to the prince: but his inheritance shall be his sons' for them. Moreover the prince shall not take of the people's inheritance by oppression, to thrust them out of their possession; but he shall give his sons inheritance out of his own possession: that my people be not scattered every man from his possession."

After he brought me through the entry, which was at the side of the gate, into the holy chambers of the priests, which looked toward the north: and, behold, there was a place on the two sides westward. Then said he unto me, "This is the place where the priests shall boil the trespass offering and the sin offering, where they shall bake the meat offering; that they bear them not out into the utter court, to sanctify the people."

Then he brought me forth into the utter court, and caused me to pass by the four corners of the court; and, behold, in every corner of the court there was a court. In the four corners of the court there were courts joined of forty cubits long and thirty broad: these four corners were of one measure. And there was a row of building round about in them, round about them four, and it was made with boiling places under the rows round about. Then said he unto me, "These are the places of them that boil, where the ministers of the house shall boil the sacrifice of the people."

Afterward he brought me again unto the door of the house; and, behold, waters issued out from under the threshold of the house eastward: for the forefront of the house stood toward the east, and the waters came down from under from the right side of the house, at the south side of the altar. Then brought he me out of the way of the gate northward, and led me about the way without unto the utter gate by the way that looketh eastward; and, behold, there ran out waters on the right side. And when the man that had the line in his hand went forth eastward, he measured a thousand cubits, and he brought me through the waters; the waters were to the ankles. Again he measured a thousand, and brought me through the waters; the waters were to the knees. Again he measured a thousand, and brought me through; the waters were to the loins. Afterward he measured a thousand; and it was a river that I could not pass over: for the waters were risen, waters to swim in, a river that could not be passed over. And he said unto me, "Son of man, hast thou seen this?"

Then he brought me, and caused me to return to the brink of the river. Now when I had returned, behold, at the bank of the river were very many trees on the one side and on the other. Then said he unto me, "These waters issue out toward the east country, and go down into the desert, and go into the sea: which being brought forth into the sea, the waters shall be healed. And it shall come to pass, that everything that liveth, which moveth, whithersoever the rivers shall come, shall live: and there shall be a very great multitude of fish, because these waters shall come thither: for they shall be healed; and every thing shall live whither the river cometh. And it shall come to pass, that the fishers shall stand upon it from En-gedi even unto En-eglaim; they shall be a place to spread forth nets; their fish shall be according to their kinds, as the fish of the great sea, exceeding many. But the miry places thereof and the marishes thereof shall not be healed; they shall be given to salt. And by the river upon the bank thereof, on this side and on that side, shall grow all trees for meat, whose leaf shall not fade, neither shall the fruit thereof be consumed: it shall bring forth new fruit according to his months, because their waters they issued out of the sanctuary: and the fruit thereof shall be for meat, and the leaf thereof for medicine."

Thus saith the Lord God; This shall be the border, whereby ye shall inherit the land according to the twelve tribes of Israel: Joseph shall have two portions. And ye shall inherit it, one as well as another: concerning the which I lifted up mine hand to give it unto your fathers: and this land shall fall unto you for inheritance. And this shall be the border of the land toward the north side, from the great sea, the way of Hethlon, as men go to Zedad; Hamath, Berothah, Sibraim, which is between the border of Damascus and the border of Hamath; Hazar-hatticon, which is by the coast of Hauran. And the border from the sea shall be Hazar-enan, the border of Damascus, and the north northward, and the border of Hamath. And this is the north side. And the east side ye shall measure from Hauran, and from Damascus, and from Gilead, and from the land of Israel by Jordan, from the border unto the east sea. And this is the east side. And the south side southward, from Tamar even to the waters of strife in Kadesh, the river to the great sea. And this is the south side southward. The west side also shall be the great sea from the border, till a man come over against Hamath. This is the west side. So shall ye divide this land unto you according to the tribes of Israel.

And it shall come to pass, that ye shall divide it by lot for an inheritance unto you, and to the strangers that sojourn among you, which shall beget children among you: and they shall be unto you as born in the country among the children of Israel; they shall have inheritance with you among the tribes of Israel. And it shall come to pass, that in what tribe the stranger sojourneth, there shall ye give him his inheritance, saith the Lord God.

Now these are the names of the tribes. From the north end to the coast of the way of Hethlon, as one goeth to Hamath, Hazar-enan, the border of Damascus northward, to the coast of Hamath, (for these are his sides east and west,) a portion for Dan. And by the border of Dan, from the east side unto the west side, a portion for Asher. And by the border of Asher, from the east side even unto the west side, a portion for Naphtali. And by the border of Naphtali, from the east side unto the west side, a portion for Manasseh. And by the border of Manasseh, from the east side unto the west side, a portion for Ephraim. And by the border of Ephraim, from the east side even unto the west side, a portion for Reuben. And by the border of Reuben, from the east side unto the west side, a portion for Judah. And by the border of Judah, from the east side unto the west side, shall be the offering which ye shall offer of five and twenty thousand reeds in breadth, and in length as one of the other parts, from the east side unto the west side: and the sanctuary shall be in the midst of it.

The oblation that ye shall offer unto the Lord shall be of five and twenty thousand in length, and of ten thousand in breadth. And for them, even for the priests, shall be this holy oblation; toward the north five and twenty thousand in length, and toward the west ten thousand in breadth, and toward the east ten thousand in breadth, and toward the south five and twenty thousand in length: and the sanctuary of the Lord shall be in the midst thereof. It shall be for the priests that are sanctified of the sons of Zadok; which have kept my charge, which went not astray when the children of Israel went astray, as the Levites went astray. And this oblation of the land that is offered shall be unto them a thing most holy by the border of the Levites.

And over against the border of the priests the Levites shall have five and twenty thousand in length, and ten thousand in breadth: all the length shall be five and twenty thousand, and the breadth ten thousand. And they shall not sell of it, neither exchange, nor alienate the firstfruits of the land: for it is holy unto the Lord.

And the five thousand, that are left in the breadth over against the five and twenty thousand, shall be a profane place for the city, for dwelling, and for suburbs: and the city shall be in the midst thereof. And these shall be the measures thereof; the north side four thousand and five hundred, and the south side four thousand and five hundred, and on the east side four thousand and five hundred, and the west side four thousand and five hundred. And the suburbs of the city shall be toward the north two hundred and fifty, and toward the south two hundred and fifty, and toward the east two hundred and fifty, and toward the west two hundred and fifty. And the residue in length over against the oblation of the holy portion shall be ten thousand eastward, and ten thousand westward: and it shall be over against the oblation of the holy portion; and the increase thereof shall be for food unto them that serve the city. And they that serve the city shall serve it out of all the tribes of Israel. All the oblation shall be five and twenty thousand by five and twenty thousand: ye shall offer the holy oblation foursquare, with the possession of the city.

And the residue shall be for the prince, on the one side and on the other of the holy oblation, and of the possession of the city, over against the five and twenty thousand of the oblation toward the east border, and westward over against the five and twenty thousand toward the west border, over against the portions for the prince: and it shall be the holy oblation; and the sanctuary of the house shall be in the midst thereof. Moreover from the possession of the Levites, and from the possession of the city, being in the midst of that which is the prince's, between the border of Judah and the border of Benjamin, shall be for the prince.

As for the rest of the tribes, from the east side unto the west side, Benjamin shall have a portion. And by the border of Benjamin, from the east side unto the west side, Simeon shall have a portion. And by the border of Simeon, from the east side unto the west side, Issachar a portion. And by the border of Issachar, from the east side unto the west side, Zebulun a portion. And by the border of Zebulun, from the east side unto the west side, Gad a portion. And by the border of Gad, at the south side southward, the border shall be even from Tamar unto the waters of strife in Kadesh, and to the river toward the great sea. This is the land which ye shall divide by lot unto the tribes of Israel for inheritance, and these are their portions, saith the Lord God.

And these are the goings out of the city on the north side, four thousand and five hundred measures. And the gates of the city shall be after the names of the tribes of Israel: three gates northward; one gate of Reuben, one gate of Judah, one gate of Levi. And at the east side four thousand and five hundred: and three gates; and one gate of Joseph, one gate of Benjamin, one gate of Dan. And at the south side four thousand and five hundred measures: and three gates; one gate of Simeon, one gate of Issachar, one gate of Zebulun. At the west side four thousand and five hundred, with their three gates; one gate of Gad, one gate of Asher, one gate of Naphtali. It was round about eighteen thousand measures: and the name of the city from that day shall be The Lord is there.

THE BOOK OF DANIEL

IN the third year of the reign of Jehoiakim king of Judah came Nebuchadnezzar king of Babylon unto Jerusalem, and besieged it. And the Lord gave Jehoiakim king of Judah into his hand, with part of the vessels of the house of God: which he carried into the land of Shinar to the house of his god; and he brought the vessels into the treasure house of his god.

And the king spake unto Ashpenaz the master of his eunuchs, that he should bring certain of the children of Israel, and of the king's seed, and of the princes; children in whom was no blemish, but well favoured, and skilful in all wisdom, and cunning in knowledge, and understanding science, and such as had ability in them to stand in the king's palace, and whom they might teach the learning and the tongue of the Chaldeans. And the king appointed them a daily provision of the king's meat, and of the wine which he drank: so nourishing them three years, that at the end thereof they might stand before the king.

. Now among these were of the children of Judah, Daniel, Hananiah, Mishael, and Azariah:

unto whom the prince of the eunuchs gave names: for he gave unto Daniel the name of Belteshazzar; and to Hananiah, of Shadrach; and to Mishael, of Meshach; and to Azariah, of Abed-nego. But Daniel purposed in his heart that he would not defile himself with the portion of the king's meat, nor with the wine which he drank: therefore he requested of the prince of the eunuchs that he might not defile himself. Now God had brought Daniel into favour and tender love with the prince of the eunuchs. And the prince of the eunuchs said unto Daniel, "I fear my lord the king, who hath appointed your meat and your drink: for why should he see your faces worse liking than the children which are of your sort? then shall ye make me endanger my head to the king" Then said Daniel to Melzar, whom the prince of the eunuchs had set over Daniel, Hananiah, Mishael, and Azariah, "Prove thy servants, I beseech thee, ten days; and let them give us pulse to eat, and water to drink Then let our countenances be looked upon before thee, and the countenance of the children that eat of the portion of the king's meat: and as thou seest, deal with thy servants." So he consented to them in this matter, and proved them ten days. And at the end of ten days their countenances appeared fairer and fatter in flesh than all the children which did eat the portion of the king's meat. Thus Melzar took away the portion of their meat, and the wine that they should drink; and gave them pulse.

As for these four children, God gave them knowledge and skill in all learning and wisdom: and Daniel had understanding in all visions and dreams. Now at the end of the days that the king had said he should bring them in, then the prince of the eunuchs brought them in before Nebuchadnezzar. And the king communed with them; and among them all was found none like Daniel, Hananiah, Mishael, and Azariah: therefore stood they before the king. And in all matters of wisdom and understanding, that the king enquired of them, he found them ten times better than all the magicians and astrologers that were in all his realm. And Daniel continued even unto the first year of king Cyrus.

And in the second year of the reign of Nebuchadnezzar Nebuchadnezzar dreamed dreams, wherewith his spirit was troubled, and his sleep brake from him. Then the king commanded to call the magicians, and the astrologers, and the sorcerers, and the Chaldeans, for to shew the king his dreams.

So they came and stood before the king. And the king said unto them, "I have dreamed a dream, and my spirit was troubled to know the dream." Then spake the Chaldeans to the king in Syriac, "O king, live for ever: tell thy servants the dream, and we will shew the interpretation."

The king answered and said to the Chaldeans, "The thing is gone from me: if ye will not make known unto me the dream, with the interpretation thereof, ye shall be cut in pieces, and your houses shall be made a dunghill. But if ye shew the dream, and the interpretation thereof, ye shall receive of me gifts and rewards and great honour: therefore shew me the dream, and the interpretation thereof." They answered again and said, "Let the king tell his servants the dream, and we will shew the interpretation of it." The king answered and said, "I know of certainty that ye would gain the time, because ye see the thing is gone from me. But if ye will not make known unto me the dream, there is but one decree for you: for ye have prepared lying and corrupt words to speak before me, till the time be changed: therefore tell me the dream, and I shall know that ye can shew me the interpretation thereof." The Chaldeans answered before the king, and said, "There is not a man upon the earth that can shew the king's matter: therefore there is no king, lord, nor ruler, that asked such things at any magician, or astrologer, or Chaldean. And it is a rare thing that the king requireth, and there is none other that can shew it before the king, except the gods, whose dwelling is not with flesh."

For this cause the king was angry and very furious, and commanded to destroy all the wise men of Babylon. And the decree went forth that the wise men should be slain; and they sought Daniel and his fellows to be slain. Then Daniel answered with counsel and wisdom to Arioch the captain of the king's guard, which was gone forth to slay the wise men of Babylon: he answered and said to Arioch the king's captain, "Why is the decree so hasty from the king?" Then Arioch made the thing known to Daniel. Then Daniel went in, and desired of the king that he would give him time, and that he would shew the king the interpretation. Then Daniel went to his house, and made the thing known to Hananiah, Mishael, and Azariah, his companions: that they would desire mercies of the God of heaven concerning this secret; that Daniel and his fellows should not perish with the rest of the wise men of Babylon.

Then was the secret revealed unto Daniel in a night vision. Then Daniel blessed the God of heaven. Daniel answered and said, "Blessed be the name of God for ever and ever: for wisdom and might are his: and he changeth the times and the seasons: he removeth kings, and setteth up kings: he giveth wisdom unto the wise, and knowledge to them that know understanding: he revealeth the deep and secret things: he knoweth what is in the darkness, and the light dwelleth with him. I thank thee, and praise thee, O thou God of my fathers, who hast given me wisdom and might, and hast made known unto me now what we desired of thee: for thou hast now made known unto us the king's matter."

Therefore Daniel went in unto Arioch, whom the king had ordained to destroy the wise men of Babylon: he went and said thus unto him; "Destroy not the wise men of Babylon: bring me in before the king, and I will shew unto the king the interpretation." Then Arioch brought in Daniel before the king in haste, and said thus unto him, "I have found a man of the captives of Judah, that will make known unto the king the interpretation." The king answered and said to Daniel, whose name was Belteshazzar, "Art thou able to make known unto me the dream which I have seen, and the interpretation thereof?" Daniel answered in the presence of the king, and said,

"The secret which the king hath demanded cannot the wise men, the astrologers, the magicians, the soothsayers, shew unto the king; but there is a God in heaven that revealeth secrets, and maketh known to the king Nebuchadnezzar what shall be in the latter days. Thy dream, and the visions of thy head upon thy bed, are these. As for thee, O king, thy thoughts came into thy mind upon thy bed, what should come to pass hereafter: and he that revealeth secrets maketh known to thee what shall come to pass. But as for me, this secret is not revealed to me for any wisdom that I have more than any living, but for their sakes that shall make known the interpretation to the king, and that thou mightest know the thoughts of thy heart.

"Thou, O king, sawest, and behold a great image. This great image, whose brightness was excellent, stood before thee; and the form thereof was terrible. This image's head was of fine gold, his breast and his arms of silver, his belly and his thighs of brass, his legs of iron, his feet part of iron and part of clay. Thou sawest till that a stone was cut out without hands, which smote the image upon his feet that were of iron and clay, and brake them to pieces. Then was the iron, the clay, the brass, the silver, and the gold, broken to pieces together, and became like the chaff of the summer threshingfloors; and the wind carried them away, that no place was found for them: and the stone that smote the image became a great mountain, and filled the whole earth.

"This is the dream; and we will tell the interpretation thereof before the king. Thou, O king, art a king of kings: for the God of heaven hath given thee a kingdom, power, and strength, and glory. And wheresoever the children of men dwell, the beasts of the field and the fowls of the heaven hath he given into thine hand, and hath made thee ruler over them all. Thou art this head of gold. And after thee shall arise another kingdom inferior to thee, and another third kingdom of brass, which shall bear rule over all the earth. And the fourth kingdom shall be strong as iron: forasmuch as iron breaketh in pieces and subdueth all things: and as iron that breaketh all these, shall it break in pieces and bruise. And whereas thou sawest the feet and toes, part of potters' clay, and part of iron, the kingdom shall be divided; but there shall be in it of the strength of the iron, forasmuch as thou sawest the iron mixed with miry clay. And as the toes of the feet were part of iron, and part of clay, so the kingdom shall be partly strong, and partly broken. And whereas thou sawest iron mixed with miry clay, they shall mingle themselves with the seed of men: but they shall not cleave one to another, even as iron is not mixed with clay. And in the days of these kings shall the God of heaven set up a kingdom, which shall never be destroyed: and the kingdom shall not be left to other people, but it shall break in pieces and consume all these kingdoms, and it shall stand for ever. Forasmuch as thou sawest that the stone was cut out of the mountain without hands, and that it brake in pieces the iron, the brass, the clay, the silver, and the gold; the great God hath made known to the king what shall come to pass hereafter: and the dream is certain, and the interpretation thereof sure."

Then the king Nebuchadnezzar fell upon his face, and worshipped Daniel, and commanded that they should offer an oblation and sweet odours unto him. The king answered unto Daniel, and said, "Of a truth it is, that your God is a God of gods, and a Lord of kings, and a revealer of secrets, seeing thou couldest reveal this secret." Then the king made Daniel a great man, and gave him many great gifts, and made him ruler over the whole province of Babylon, and chief of the governors over all the wise men of Babylon. Then Daniel requested of the king, and he set Shadrach, Meshach, and Abed-nego, over the affairs of the province of Babylon: but Daniel sat in the gate of the king.

NEBUCHADNEZZAR the king made an image of gold, whose height was threescore cubits, and the breadth thereof six cubits: he set it up in the plain of Dura, in the province of Babylon. Then Nebuchadnezzar the king sent to gather together the princes, the governors, and the captains, the judges, the treasurers, the counsellors, the sheriffs, and all the rulers of the provinces, to come to the dedication of the image which Nebuchadnezzar the king had set up.

Then the princes, the governors, and captains, the judges, the treasurers, the counsellors, the sheriffs, and all the rulers of the provinces, were gathered together unto the dedication of the image that Nebuchadnezzar the king had set up; and they stood before the image that Nebuchadnezzar had set up. Then an herald cried aloud, "To you it is commanded, O people, nations, and languages, that at what time ye hear the sound of the cornet, flute, harp, sackbut, psaltery, dulcimer, and all kinds of music, ye fall down and worship the golden image that Nebuchadnezzar the king hath set up: and whoso falleth not down and worshippeth shall the same hour be cast into the midst of a burning fiery furnace." Therefore at that time, when all the people heard the sound of the cornet, flute, harp, sackbut, psaltery, and all kinds of music, all the people, the nations, and the languages, fell down and worshipped the golden image that Nebuchadnezzar the king had set up.

Wherefore at that time certain Chaldeans came near, and accused the Jews. They spake and said to the king Nebuchadnezzar, "O king, live for ever. Thou, O king, hast made a decree, that every man that shall hear the sound of the cornet, flute, harp, sackbut, psaltery, and dulcimer, and all kinds of music, shall fall down and worship the golden image: and whoso falleth not down and worshippeth, that he should be cast into the midst of a burning fiery furnace. There are certain Jews whom thou hast set over the affairs of the province of Babylon, Shadrach, Meshach, and Abed-nego; these men, O king, have not regarded thee: they serve not thy gods, nor worship the golden image which thou hast set up."

Then Nebuchadnezzar in his rage and fury commanded to bring Shadrach, Meshach, and Abed-nego. Then they brought these men before the king. Nebuchadnezzar spake and said unto them, "Is it true, O Shadrach, Meshach, and Abed-nego, do not ye serve my gods, nor worship the golden image which I have set up? Now if ye be ready that at what time ye hear the sound of the cornet, flute, harp, sackbut, psaltery, and dulcimer, and all kinds of music, ye fall down and worship the image which I have made; well: but if ye worship not, ye shall be cast the same hour into the midst of a burning fiery furnace; and who is that God that shall deliver you out of my hands?"

Shadrach, Meshach, and Abed-nego, answered and said to the king, "O Nebuchadnezzar, we are not careful to answer thee in this matter. If it be so, our God whom we serve is able to deliver us from the burning fiery furnace, and he will deliver us out of thine hand, O king. But if not, be it known unto thee, O king, that we will not serve thy gods, nor worship the golden image which thou hast set up." Then was Nebuchadnezzar full of fury, and the form of his visage was changed against Shadrach, Meshach, and Abed-nego: therefore he spake, and commanded that they should heat the furnace one seven times more than it was wont to be heated. And he commanded the most mighty men that were in his army to bind Shadrach, Meshach, and Abed-nego, and to cast them into the burning fiery furnace.

Then these men were bound in their coats, their hosen, and their hats, and their other garments, and were cast into the midst of the burning fiery furnace. Therefore because the king's commandment was urgent, and the furnace exceeding hot, the flame of the fire slew those men that took up Shadrach, Meshach, and Abed-nego. And these three men, Shadrach, Meshach, and Abed-nego, fell down bound into the midst of the burning fiery furnace.

Then Nebuchadnezzar the king was astonied, and rose up in haste, and spake, and said unto his counsellors, "Did not we cast three men bound into the midst of the fire?" They answered and said unto the king, "True, O king." He answered and said, "Lo, I see four men loose, walking in the midst of the fire, and they have no hurt; and the form of the fourth is like the Son of God." Then Nebuchadnezzar came near to the mouth of the burning fiery furnace, and spake, and said, "Shadrach, Meshach, and Abed-nego, ye servants of the most high God, come forth, and come hither."

Then Shadrach, Meshach, and Abed-nego, came forth of the midst of the fire. And the princes, governors, and captains, and the king's counsellors, being gathered together, saw these men, upon whose bodies the fire had no power, nor was an hair of their head singed, neither were their coats changed, nor the smell of fire had passed on them. Then Nebuchadnezzar spake, and said, "Blessed be the God of Shadrach, Meshach, and Abed-nego, who hath sent his Angel, and delivered his servants that trusted in him, and have changed the king's word, and yielded their bodies, that they might not serve nor worship any god, except their own God. Therefore I make a decree, That every people, nation, and language, which speak anything amiss against the God of Shadrach, Meshach, and Abed-nego, shall be cut in pieces, and their houses shall be made a dunghill: because there is no other God that can deliver after this sort."

Then the king promoted Shadrach, Meshach, and Abed-nego, in the province of Babylon.

"NEBUCHADNEZZAR the king, unto all people, nations, and languages, that dwell in all the earth; Peace be multiplied unto you.

"I thought it good to shew the signs and wonders that the high God hath wrought toward me. How great are his signs! and how mighty are his wonders! his kingdom is an everlasting kingdom, and his dominion is from generation to generation.

"I Nebuchadnezzar was at rest in mine house, and flourishing in my palace: I saw a dream which made me afraid, and the thoughts upon my bed and the visions of my head troubled me. Therefore made I a decree to bring in all the wise men of Babylon before me, that they might make known unto me the interpretation of the dream. Then came in the magicians, the astrologers, the Chaldeans, and the soothsayers: and I told the dream before them; but they did not make known unto me the interpretation thereof. But at the last Daniel came in before me, whose name was Belteshazzar, according to the name of my god, and in whom is the spirit of the holy gods: and before him I told the dream, saying, O Belteshazzar, master of the magicians, because I know that the spirit of the holy gods is in thee, and no secret troubleth thee, tell me the visions of my dream that I have seen, and the interpretation thereof.

"Thus were the visions of mine head in my bed; I saw, and behold a tree in the midst of the earth, and the height thereof was great. The tree grew, and was strong, and the height thereof reached unto heaven, and the sight thereof to the end of all the earth: the leaves thereof were fair, and the fruit thereof much, and in it was meat for all: the beasts of the field had shadow under it, and the fowls of the heaven dwelt in the boughs thereof, and all flesh was fed of it.

"I saw in the visions of my head upon my bed, and, behold, a Watcher and an Holy One came down from heaven; he cried aloud, and said thus, Hew down the tree, and cut off his branches, shake off his leaves, and scatter his fruit: let the beasts get away from under it, and the fowls from his branches: nevertheless leave the stump of his roots in the earth, even with a band of iron and brass, in the tender grass of the field; and let it be wet with the dew of heaven, and let his portion be with the beasts in the grass of the earth: let his heart be changed from man's, and let a beast's heart be given unto him; and let seven times pass over him. This matter is by the decree of the Watchers, and the demand by the word of the Holy Ones: to the intent that the living may know that the Most High ruleth in the kingdom of men, and giveth it to whomsoever he will, and setteth up over it the basest of men.

"This dream I king Nebuchadnezzar have seen. Now thou, O Belteshazzar, declare the interpretation thereof, forasmuch as all the wise men of my kingdom are not able to make known unto me the interpretation: but thou art able; for the spirit of the holy gods is in thee.

"Then Daniel, whose name was Belteshazzar, was astonied for one hour, and his thoughts troubled him. The king spake, and said, Belteshazzar, let not the dream, or the interpretation thereof, trouble thee. Belteshazzar answered and said, My lord, the dream be to them that hate thee, and the interpretation thereof to thine enemies! The tree that thou sawest, which grew, and was strong, whose height reached unto the heaven, and the sight thereof to all the earth; whose leaves were fair, and the fruit thereof much, and in it was meat for all; under which the beasts of the field dwelt, and upon whose branches the fowls of the heaven had their habitation: it is thou, O king, that art grown and become strong: for thy greatness is grown, and reacheth unto heaven, and thy dominion to the end of the earth.

"And whereas the king saw a Watcher and an Holy One coming down from heaven, and saying, Hew the tree down, and destroy it; yet leave the stump of the roots thereof in the earth, even with a band of iron and brass, in the tender grass of the field; and let it be wet with the dew of heaven, and let his portion be with the beasts of the field, till seven times pass over him;

this is the interpretation, O king, and this is the decree of the Most High, which is come upon my lord the king: that they shall drive thee from men, and thy dwelling shall be with the beasts of the field, and they shall make thee to eat grass as oxen, and they shall wet thee with the dew of heaven, and seven times shall pass over thee, till thou know that the Most High ruleth in the kingdom of men, and giveth it to whomsoever he will. And whereas they commanded to leave the stump of the tree roots; thy kingdom shall be sure unto thee, after that thou shalt have known that the heavens do rule. Wherefore, O king, let my counsel be acceptable unto thee, and break off thy sins by righteousness, and thine iniquities by shewing mercy to the poor; if it may be a lengthening of thy tranquillity.

"All this came upon the king Nebuchadnezzar. At the end of twelve months he walked in the palace of the kingdom of Babylon. The king spake, and said, Is not this great Babylon, that I have built for the house of the kingdom by the might of my power, and for the honour of my majesty?

"While the word was in the king's mouth, there fell a voice from heaven, saying, O king Nebuchadnezzar, to thee it is spoken; the kingdom is departed from thee. And they shall drive thee from men, and thy dwelling shall be with the beasts of the field: they shall make thee to eat grass as oxen, and seven times shall pass over thee, until thou know that the Most High ruleth in the kingdom of men, and giveth it to whomsoever he will. The same hour was the thing fulfilled upon Nebuchadnezzar: and he was driven from men, and did eat grass as oxen, and his body was wet with the dew of heaven, till his hairs were grown like eagles' feathers, and his nails like birds' claws. And at the end of the days I Nebuchadnezzar lifted up mine eyes unto heaven, and mine understanding returned unto me, and I blessed the Most High, and I praised and honoured him that liveth for ever, whose dominion is an everlasting dominion, and his kingdom is from generation to generation: and all the inhabitants of the earth are reputed as nothing: and he doeth according to his will in the army of heaven, and among the inhabitants of the earth: and none can stay his hand, or say unto him, What doest thou? At the same time my reason returned unto me; and for the glory of my kingdom, mine honour and brightness returned unto me; and my counsellors and my lords sought unto me; and I was established in my kingdom, and excellent majesty was added unto me.

"Now I Nebuchadnezzar praise and extol and honour the King of heaven, all whose works are truth, and his ways judgment: and those that walk in pride he is able to abase."

BELSHAZZAR the king made a great feast to a thousand of his lords, and drank wine before the thousand. Belshazzar, whiles he tasted the wine, commanded to bring the golden and silver vessels which his father Nebuchadnezzar had taken out of the temple which was in Jerusalem; that the king, and his princes, his wives, and his concubines, might drink therein. Then they brought the golden vessels that were taken out of the temple of the house of God which was at Jerusalem; and the king, and his princes, his wives, and his concubines, drank in them. They drank wine, and praised the gods of gold, and of silver, of brass, of iron, of wood, and of stone.

In the same hour came forth fingers of a man's hand, and wrote over against the candlestick upon the plaster of the wall of the king's palace: and the king saw the part of the hand that wrote. Then the king's countenance was changed, and his thoughts troubled him, so that the joints of his loins were loosed, and his knees smote one against another. The king cried aloud to bring in the astrologers, the Chaldeans, and the soothsayers. And the king spake, and said to the wise men of Babylon, "Whosoever shall read this writing, and shew me the interpretation thereof, shall be clothed with scarlet, and have a chain of gold about his neck, and shall be the third ruler in the kingdom." Then came in all the king's wise men: but they could not read the writing, nor make known to the king the interpretation thereof. Then was king Belshazzar greatly troubled, and his countenance was changed in him, and his lords were astonied.

Now the queen by reason of the words of the king and his lords came into the banquet house: and the queen spake and said, "O king, live for ever: let not thy thoughts trouble thee, nor let thy countenance be changed: there is a man in thy kingdom, in whom is the spirit of the holy gods; and in the days of thy father light and understanding and wisdom, like the wisdom of the gods, was found in him; whom the king Nebuchadnezzar thy father, the king, I say, thy father, made master of the magicians, astrologers, Chaldeans, and soothsayers; forasmuch as an excellent spirit, and knowledge, and understanding, interpreting of dreams, and shewing of hard sentences, and dissolving of doubts, were found in the same Daniel, whom the king named Belteshazzar: now let Daniel be called, and he will shew the interpretation."

Then was Daniel brought in before the king. And the king spake and said unto Daniel, "Art thou that Daniel, which art of the children of the captivity of Judah, whom the king my father brought out of Jewry? I have even heard of thee, that the spirit of the gods is in thee, and that light and understanding and excellent wisdom is found in thee. And now the wise men, the astrologers, have been brought in before me, that they should read this writing, and make known unto me the interpretation thereof: but they could not shew the interpretation of the thing: and I have heard of thee, that thou canst make interpretations, and dissolve doubts: now if thou canst read the writing, and make known to me the interpretation thereof, thou shalt be clothed with scarlet, and have a chain of gold about thy neck, and shalt be the third ruler in the kingdom."

Then Daniel answered and said before the king, "Let thy gifts be to thyself, and give thy rewards to another; yet I will read the writing unto the king, and make known to him the interpretation. O thou king, the most high God gave Nebuchadnezzar thy father a kingdom, and majesty, and glory, and honour: and for the majesty that he gave him, all people, nations, and languages, trembled and feared before him: whom he would he slew; and whom he would he kept alive; and whom he would he set up; and whom he would he put down. But when his heart was lifted up, and his mind hardened in pride, he was deposed from his kingly throne, and they took his glory from him: and he was driven from the sons of men; and his heart was made like the beasts, and his dwelling was with the wild asses: they fed him with grass like oxen, and his body was wet with the dew of heaven; till he knew that the most high God ruled in the kingdom of men, and that he appointeth over it whomsoever he will.

"And thou his son, O Belshazzar, hast not humbled thine heart, though thou knewest all this; but hast lifted up thyself against the Lord of heaven; and they have brought the vessels of his house before thee, and thou, and thy lords, thy wives, and thy concubines, have drunk wine in them; and thou hast praised the gods of silver and gold, of brass, iron, wood, and stone, which see not, nor hear, nor know: and the God in whose hand thy breath is, and whose are all thy ways, hast thou not glorified:" (then was the part of the hand sent from him; and this writing was written. And this is the writing that was written, Mene, Mene, Tekel, Upharsin:) "this is the interpretation of the thing: Mene; God hath numbered thy kingdom, and finished it. Tekel; Thou art weighed in the balances, and art found wanting. Peres; Thy kingdom is divided, and given to the Medes and Persians."

Then commanded Belshazzar, and they clothed Daniel with scarlet, and put a chain of gold about his neck, and made a proclamation concerning him, that he should be the third ruler in the kingdom.

In that night was Belshazzar the king of the Chaldeans slain. And Darius the Median took the kingdom, being about threescore and two years old.

IT PLEASED Darius to set over the kingdom an hundred and twenty princes, which should be over the whole kingdom; and over these three presidents, of whom Daniel was first: that the princes might give accounts unto them, and the king should have no damage. Then this Daniel was preferred above the presidents and princes, because an excellent spirit was in him; and the king thought to set him over the whole realm.

Then the presidents and princes sought to find occasion against Daniel concerning the kingdom; but they could find none occasion nor fault; forasmuch as he was faithful, neither was there any error or fault found in him. Then said these men, "We shall not find any occasion against this Daniel, except we find it against him concerning the law of his God." Then these presidents and princes assembled together to the king, and said thus unto him, "King Darius, live for ever. All the presidents of the kingdom, the governors, and the princes, the counsellors, and the captains, have consulted together to establish a royal statute, and to make a firm decree, that whosoever shall ask a petition of any God or man for thirty days, save of thee, O king, he shall be cast into the den of lions. Now, O king, establish the decree, and sign the writing, that it be not changed, according to the law of the Medes and Persians, which altereth not." Wherefore king Darius signed the writing and the decree.

Now when Daniel knew that the writing was signed, he went into his house; and his windows being open in his chamber toward Jerusalem, he kneeled upon his knees three times a day, and prayed, and gave thanks before his God, as he did aforetime. Then these men assembled, and found Daniel praying and making supplication before his God. Then they came near, and spake before the king concerning the king's decree; "Hast thou not signed a decree, that every man that shall ask a petition of any God or man within thirty days, save of thee, O king, shall be cast into the den of lions?" The king answered and said, "The thing is true, according to the law of the Medes and Persians, which altereth not." Then answered they and said before the king, "That Daniel, which is of the children of the captivity of Judah, regardeth not thee, O king, nor the decree that thou hast signed, but maketh his petition three times a day."

Then the king, when he heard these words, was sore displeased with himself, and set his heart on Daniel to deliver him: and he laboured till the going down of the sun to deliver him. Then these men assembled unto the king, and said unto the king, "Know, O king, that the law of the Medes and Persians is, that no decree nor statute which the king establisheth may be changed." Then the king commanded, and they brought Daniel, and cast him into the den of lions. Now the king spake and said unto Daniel, "Thy God whom thou servest continually, he will deliver thee." And a stone was brought, and laid upon the mouth of the den; and the king sealed it with his own signet, and with the signet of his lords; that the purpose might not be changed concerning Daniel.

Then the king went to his palace, and passed the night fasting: neither were instruments of music brought before him: and his sleep went from him. Then the king arose very early in the morning, and went in haste unto the den of lions. And when he came to the den, he cried with a lamentable voice unto Daniel: and the king spake and said to Daniel, "O Daniel, servant of the living God, is thy God, whom thou servest continually, able to deliver thee from the lions?" Then said Daniel unto the king, "O king, live for ever: my God hath sent his Angel, and hath shut the lions' mouths, that they have not hurt me: forasmuch as before him innocency was found in me; and also before thee, O king, have I done no hurt." Then was the king exceeding glad for him, and commanded that they should take Daniel up out of the den. So Daniel was taken up out of the den, and no manner of hurt was found upon him, because he believed in his God. And the king commanded, and they brought those men which had accused Daniel, and they cast them into the den of lions, them, their children, and their wives; and the lions had the mastery of them, and brake all their bones in pieces or ever they came at the bottom of the den.

Then king Darius wrote unto all people, nations, and languages, that dwell in all the earth; "Peace be multiplied unto you. I make a decree, that in every dominion of my kingdom men tremble and fear before the God of Daniel: for he is the living God, and stedfast for ever, and his kingdom that which shall not be destroyed, and his dominion shall be even unto the end. He delivereth and rescueth, and he worketh signs and wonders in heaven and in earth, who hath delivered Daniel from the power of the lions."

So this Daniel prospered in the reign of Darius, and in the reign of Cyrus the Persian.

IN THE first year of Belshazzar king of Babylon Daniel had a dream and visions of his head upon his bed: then he wrote the dream, and told the sum of the matters. Daniel spake and said,

I saw in my vision by night, and, behold, the four winds of the heaven strove upon the great sea. And four great beasts came up from the sea, diverse one from another. The first was like a lion, and had eagle's wings: I beheld till the wings thereof were plucked, and it was lifted up from the earth, and made stand upon the feet as a man, and a man's heart was given to it. And behold another beast, a second, like to a bear, and it raised up itself on one side, and it had three ribs in the mouth of it between the teeth of it: and they said thus unto it, "Arise, devour much flesh." After this I beheld, and lo another, like a leopard, which had upon the back of it four wings of a fowl; the beast had also four heads; and dominion was given to it. After this I saw in the night visions, and behold a fourth beast, dreadful and terrible, and strong exceedingly; and it had great iron teeth: it devoured and brake in pieces, and stamped the residue with the feet of it: and it was diverse from all the beasts that were before it; and it had ten horns. I considered the horns, and, behold, there came up among them another little horn, before whom there were three of the first horns plucked up by the roots: and, behold, in this horn were eyes like the eyes of man, and a mouth speaking great things.

I beheld till the thrones were cast down, and the Ancient of Days did sit, whose garment was white as snow, and the hair of his head like the pure wool: his throne was like the fiery flame, and his wheels as burning fire. A fiery stream issued and came forth from before him: thousand thousands ministered unto him, and ten thousand times ten thousand stood before him: the judgment was set, and the books were opened. I beheld then because of the voice of the great words which the horn spake: I beheld even till the beast was slain, and his body destroyed, and given to the burning flame. As concerning the rest of the beasts, they had their dominion taken away: yet their lives were prolonged for a season and time. I saw in the night visions, and, behold, one like the Son of man came with the clouds of heaven, and came to the Ancient of Days, and they brought him near before him. And there was given him dominion, and glory, and a kingdom, that all people, nations, and languages, should serve him: his dominion is an everlasting dominion, which shall not pass away, and his kingdom that which shall not be destroyed.

I Daniel was grieved in my spirit in the midst of my body, and the visions of my head troubled me. I came near unto one of them that stood by, and asked him the truth of all this. So he told me, and made me know the interpretation of the things: "These great beasts, which are four, are four kings, which shall arise out of the earth. But the saints of the Most High shall take the kingdom, and possess the kingdom for ever, even for ever and ever."

Then I would know the truth of the fourth beast, which was diverse from all the others, exceeding dreadful, whose teeth were of iron, and his nails of brass; which devoured, brake in pieces, and stamped the residue with his feet; and of the ten horns that were in his head, and of the other which came up, and before whom three fell; even of that horn that had eyes, and a mouth that spake very great things, whose look was more stout than his fellows. I beheld, and the same horn made war with the saints, and prevailed against them; until the Ancient of Days came, and judgment was given to the saints of the Most High; and the time came that the saints possessed the kingdom.

Thus he said, "The fourth beast shall be the fourth kingdom upon earth, which shall be diverse from all kingdoms, and shall devour the whole earth, and shall tread it down, and break it in pieces. And the ten horns out of this kingdom are ten kings that shall arise: and another shall rise after them; and he shall be diverse from the first, and he shall subdue three kings. And he shall speak great words against the Most High, and shall wear out the saints of the Most High, and think to change times and laws: and they shall be given into his hand until a time and times and the dividing of time. But the judgment shall sit, and they shall take away his dominion, to consume and to destroy it unto the end. And the kingdom and dominion, and the greatness of the kingdom under the whole heaven, shall be given to the people of the saints of the Most High, whose kingdom is an everlasting kingdom, and all dominions shall serve and obey him."

Hitherto is the end of the matter. As for me Daniel, my cogitations much troubled me, and my countenance changed in me: but I kept the matter in my heart.

In the third year of the reign of king Belshazzar a vision appeared unto me, even unto me Daniel, after that which appeared unto me at the first. And I saw in a vision; and it came to pass, when I saw, that I was at Shushan in the palace, which is in the province of Elam; and I saw in a vision, and I was by the river of Ulai. Then I lifted up mine eyes, and saw, and, behold, there stood before the river a ram which had two horns: and the two horns were high; but one was higher than the other, and the higher came up last. I saw the ram pushing westward, and northward, and southward; so that no beasts might stand before him, neither was there any that could deliver out of his hand; but he did according to his will, and became great.

And as I was considering, behold, an he goat came from the west on the face of the whole earth, and touched not the ground: and the goat had a notable horn between his eyes. And he came to the ram that had two horns, which I had seen standing before the river, and ran unto him in the fury of his power. And I saw him come close unto the ram, and he was moved with choler against him, and smote the ram, and brake his two horns: and there was no power in the ram to stand before him, but he cast him down to the ground, and stamped upon him: and there was none that could deliver the ram out of his hand. Therefore the he goat waxed very great: and when he was strong, the great horn was broken; and for it came up four notable ones toward the four winds of heaven.

And out of one of them came forth a little horn, which waxed exceeding great, toward the south, and toward the east, and toward the pleasant land. And it waxed great, even to the host of heaven; and it cast down some of the host and of the stars to the ground, and stamped upon them. Yea, he magnified himself even to the prince of the host, and by him the daily sacrifice was taken away, and the place of his sanctuary was cast down. And an host was given him against the daily sacrifice by reason of transgression, and it cast down the truth to the ground; and it practised, and prospered.

Then I heard one saint speaking, and another saint said unto that certain saint which spake, "How long shall be the vision concerning the daily sacrifice, and the transgression of desolation, to give both the sanctuary and the host to be trodden under foot?" And he said unto me, "Unto two thousand and three hundred days; then shall the sanctuary be cleansed."

And it came to pass, when I, even I Daniel, had seen the vision, and sought for the meaning, then, behold, there stood before me as the appearance of a man. And I heard a man's voice between the banks of Ulai, which called, and said, "Gabriel, make this man to understand the vision." So he came near where I stood: and when he came, I was afraid, and fell upon my face: but he said unto me, "Understand, O son of man: for at the time of the end shall be the vision."

Now as he was speaking with me, I was in a deep sleep on my face toward the ground: but he touched me, and set me upright. And he said, "Behold, I will make thee know what shall be in the last end of the indignation: for at the time appointed the end shall be. The ram which thou sawest having two horns are the kings of Media and Persia. And the rough goat is the king of Grecia: and the great horn that is between his eyes is the first king. Now that being broken, whereas four stood up for it, four kingdoms shall stand up out of the nation, but not in his power And in the latter time of their kingdom, when the transgressors are come to the full, a king of fierce countenance, and understanding dark sentences, shall stand up. And his power shall be mighty, but not by his own power: and he shall destroy wonderfully, and shall prosper, and practise, and shall destroy the mighty and the holy people. And through his policy also he shall cause craft to prosper in his hand; and he shall magnify himself in his heart, and by peace shall destroy many: he shall also stand up against the Prince of princes; but he shall be broken without hand. And the vision of the evening and the morning which was told is true: wherefore shut thou up the vision; for it shall be for many days."

And I Daniel fainted, and was sick certain days; afterward I rose up, and did the king's business; and I was astonished at the vision, but none understood it.

In the first year of Darius the son of Ahasuerus, of the seed of the Medes, which was made king over the realm of the Chaldeans; in the first year of his reign I Daniel understood by books the number of the years, whereof the word of the Lord came to Jeremiah the prophet, that he would accomplish seventy years in the desolations of Jerusalem. And I set my face unto the Lord God, to seek by prayer and supplications, with fasting, and sackcloth, and ashes.

And I prayed unto the Lord my God, and made my confession, and said, "O Lord, the great and dreadful God, keeping the covenant and mercy to them that love him, and to them that keep his commandments; we have sinned, and have committed iniquity, and have done wickedly, and have rebelled, even by departing from thy precepts and from thy judgments: neither have we hearkened unto thy servants the prophets, which spake in thy name to our kings, our princes, and our fathers, and to all the people of the land. O Lord, righteousness belongeth unto thee, but unto us confusion of faces, as at this day; to the men of Judah, and to the inhabitants of Jerusalem, and unto all Israel, that are near, and that are far off, through all the countries whither thou hast driven them, because of their trespass that they have trespassed against thee. O Lord, to us belongeth confusion of face, to our kings, to our princes, and to our fathers, because we have sinned against thee. To the Lord our God belong mercies and forgivenesses, though we have rebelled against him; neither have we obeyed the voice of the Lord our God, to walk in his laws, which he set before us by his servants the prophets. Yea, all Israel have transgressed thy law, even by departing, that they might not obey thy voice; therefore the curse is poured upon us, and the oath that is written in the law of Moses the servant of God, because we have sinned against him. And he hath confirmed his words, which he spake against us, and against our judges that judged us, by bringing upon us a great evil: for under the whole heaven hath not been done as hath been done upon Jerusalem. As it is written in the law of Moses, all this evil is come upon us: yet made we not our prayer before the Lord our God, that we might turn from our iniquities, and understand thy truth. Therefore hath the Lord watched upon the evil, and brought it upon us: for the Lord our God is righteous in all his works which he doeth: for we obeyed not his voice.

"And now, O Lord our God, that hast brought thy people forth out of the land of Egypt with a mighty hand, and hast gotten thee renown, as at this day; we have sinned, we have done wickedly. O Lord, according to all thy righteousness, I beseech thee, let thine anger and thy fury be turned away from thy city Jerusalem, thy holy mountain: because for our sins, and for the iniquities of our fathers, Jerusalem and thy people are become a reproach to all that are about us. Now therefore, O our God, hear the prayer of thy servant, and his supplications, and cause thy face to shine upon thy sanctuary that is desolate, for the Lord's sake. O my God, incline thine ear, and hear; open thine eyes, and behold our desolations, and the city which is called by thy name: for we do not present our supplications before thee for our righteousnesses, but for thy great mercies. O Lord, hear; O Lord, forgive; O Lord, hearken and do; defer not, for thine own sake, O my God: for thy city and thy people are called by thy name."

And whiles I was speaking, and praying, and confessing my sin and the sin of my people Israel, and presenting my supplication before the Lord my God for the holy mountain of my God; yea, whiles I was speaking in prayer, even the man Gabriel, whom I had seen in the vision at the beginning, being caused to fly swiftly, touched me about the time of the evening oblation. And he informed me, and talked with me, and said, "O Daniel, I am now come forth to give thee skill and understanding. At the beginning of thy supplications the commandment came forth, and I am come to shew thee; for thou art greatly beloved: therefore understand the matter, and consider the vision. Seventy weeks are determined upon thy people and upon thy holy city, to finish the transgression, and to make an end of sins, and to make reconciliation for iniquity, and to bring in everlasting righteousness, and to seal up the vision and prophecy, and to anoint the Most Holy.

"Know therefore and understand, that from the going forth of the commandment to restore and to build Jerusalem unto the Messiah the Prince shall be seven weeks, and threescore and two weeks: the street shall be built again, and the wall, even in troublous times. And after threescore and two weeks shall Messiah be cut off, but not for himself: and the people of the prince that shall come shall destroy the city and the sanctuary; and the end thereof shall be with a flood, and unto the end of the war desolations are determined. And he shall confirm the covenant with many for one week: and in the midst of the week he shall cause the sacrifice and the oblation to cease, and for the overspreading of abominations he shall make it desolate, even until the consummation, and that determined shall be poured upon the desolate."

In the third year of Cyrus king of Persia a thing was revealed unto Daniel, whose name was called Belteshazzar; and the thing was true, but the time appointed was long: and he understood the thing, and had understanding of the vision.

In those days I Daniel was mourning three full weeks. I ate no pleasant bread, neither came flesh nor wine in my mouth, neither did I anoint myself at all, till three whole weeks were fulfilled. And in the four and twentieth day of the first month, as I was by the side of the great river, which is Hiddekel, then I lifted up mine eyes, and looked, and behold a certain man clothed in linen, whose loins were girded with fine gold of Uphaz: his body also was like the beryl, and his face as the appearance of lightning, and his eyes as lamps of fire, and his arms and his feet like in colour to polished brass, and the voice of his words like the voice of a multitude. And I Daniel alone saw the vision: for the men that were with me saw not the vision; but a great quaking fell upon them, so that they fled to hide themselves. Therefore I was left alone, and saw this great vision, and there remained no strength in me: for my comeliness was turned in me into corruption, and I retained no strength. Yet heard I the voice of his words: and when I heard the voice of his words, then was I in a deep sleep on my face, and my face toward the ground.

And, behold, an hand touched me, which set me upon my knees and upon the palms of my hands. And he said unto me, "O Daniel, a man greatly beloved, understand the words that I speak unto thee, and stand upright: for unto

thee am I now sent." And when he had spoken
this word unto me, I stood trembling. Then
said he unto me, "Fear not, Daniel: for from
the first day that thou didst set thine heart to
understand, and to chasten thyself before thy
God, thy words were heard, and I am come for
thy words. But the prince of the kingdom of
Persia withstood me one and twenty days: but,
lo, Michael, one of the chief princes, came to
help me; and I remained there with the kings
of Persia. Now I am come to make thee understand what shall befall thy people in the latter
days: for yet the vision is for many days."

And when he had spoken such words unto
me, I set my face toward the ground, and I
became dumb. And, behold, one like the
similitude of the sons of men touched my lips:
then I opened my mouth, and spake, and said
unto him that stood before me, "O my lord,
by the vision my sorrows are turned upon me,
and I have retained no strength. For how can
the servant of this my lord talk with this my
lord? for as for me, straightway there remained
no strength in me, neither is there breath left
in me."

Then there came again and touched me one
like the appearance of a man, and he strengthened me, and said, "O man greatly beloved, fear
not : peace be unto thee, be strong, yea, be
strong." And when he had spoken unto me, I

was strengthened, and said, "Let my lord speak; for thou hast strengthened me." Then said he, "Knowest thou wherefore I come unto thee? and now will I return to fight with the prince of Persia: and when I am gone forth, lo, the prince of Grecia shall come. But I will shew thee that which is noted in the scripture of truth: and there is none that holdeth with me in these things, but Michael your prince. Also I in the first year of Darius the Mede, even I, stood to confirm and to strengthen him.

"And now will I shew thee the truth. Behold, there shall stand up yet three kings in Persia; and the fourth shall be far richer than they all: and by his strength through his riches he shall stir up all against the realm of Grecia. And a mighty king shall stand up, that shall rule with great dominion, and do according to his will. And when he shall stand up, his kingdom shall be broken, and shall be divided toward the four winds of heaven; and not to his posterity, nor according to his dominion which he ruled: for his kingdom shall be plucked up, even for others beside those.

"And the king of the south shall be strong, and one of his princes; and he shall be strong above him, and have dominion; his dominion shall be a great dominion. And in the end of years they shall join themselves together; for the king's daughter of the south shall come to the king of the north to make an agreement: but she shall not retain the power of the arm; neither shall he stand, nor his arm: but she shall be given up, and they that brought her, and he that begat her, and he that strengthened her in these times. But out of a branch of her roots shall one stand up in his estate, which shall come with an army, and shall enter into the fortress of the king of the north, and shall deal against them, and shall prevail: and shall also carry captives into Egypt their gods, with their princes, and with their precious vessels of silver and of gold; and he shall continue more years than the king of the north. So the king of the south shall come into his kingdom, and shall return into his own land.

"But his sons shall be stirred up, and shall assemble a multitude of great forces: and one shall certainly come, and overflow, and pass through: then shall he return, and be stirred up, even to his fortress. And the king of the south shall be moved with choler, and shall come forth and fight with him, even with the king of the north: and he shall set forth a great multitude; but the multitude shall be given into his hand. And when he hath taken away the multitude, his heart shall be lifted up; and he shall cast down many ten thousands: but he shall not be strengthened by it. For the king of the north shall return, and shall set forth a multitude greater than the former, and shall certainly come after certain years with a great army and with much riches. And in those times there shall many stand up against the king of the south: also the robbers of thy people shall exalt themselves to establish the vision; but they shall fall. So the king of the north shall come, and cast up a mount, and take the most fenced cities: and the arms of the south shall not withstand, neither his chosen people, neither shall there be any strength to withstand. But he that cometh against him shall do according to his own will, and none shall stand before him: and he shall stand in the glorious land, which by his hand shall be consumed. He shall also set his face to enter with the strength of his whole kingdom, and upright ones with him; thus shall he do: and he shall give him the daughter of women, corrupting her: but she shall not stand on his side, neither be for him. After this shall he turn his face unto the isles, and shall take many: but a prince for his own behalf shall cause the reproach offered by him to cease; without his own reproach he shall cause it to turn upon him. Then he shall turn his face toward the fort of his own land: but he shall stumble and fall, and not be found.

"Then shall stand up in his estate a raiser of taxes in the glory of the kingdom: but within few days he shall be destroyed, neither in anger, nor in battle. And in his estate shall stand up a vile person, to whom they shall not give the honour of the kingdom: but he shall come in peaceably, and obtain the kingdom by flatteries. And with the arms of a flood shall they be overflown from before him, and shall be broken; yea, also the prince of the covenant. And after the league made with him he shall work deceitfully: for he shall come up, and shall become strong with a small people. He shall enter peaceably even upon the fattest places of the province; and he shall do that which his fathers have not done, nor his fathers' fathers; he shall scatter among them the prey, and spoil, and riches: yea, and he shall forecast his devices against the strong holds, even for a time. And he shall stir up his power and his courage against the king of the south with a great army; and the king of the south shall be stirred up to battle with a very great and mighty army; but he shall not stand: for they shall forecast devices against him. Yea, they that feed of the portion of his meat shall destroy him, and his army shall overflow: and many shall fall down slain. And both these kings' hearts shall be to do mischief, and they shall speak lies at one table; but it shall not prosper: for yet the end shall be at the time appointed. Then shall he return into his land with great riches; and his heart shall be against the holy covenant; and he shall do exploits, and return to his own land.

"At the time appointed he shall return, and come toward the south; but it shall not be as the former, or as the latter. For the ships of Chittim shall come against him: therefore he shall be grieved, and return, and have indignation against the holy covenant: so shall he do; he shall even return, and have intelligence with them that forsake the holy covenant. And arms shall stand on his part, and they shall pollute the sanctuary of strength, and shall take away the daily sacrifice, and they shall place the abomination that maketh desolate. And such as do wickedly against the covenant shall be corrupt by flatteries: but the people that do know their God shall be strong, and do exploits. And they that understand among the people shall instruct many: yet they shall fall by the sword, and by flame, by captivity, and by spoil, many days. Now when they shall fall, they shall be holpen with a little help: but many shall cleave to them with flatteries. And some of them of understanding shall fall, to try them, and to purge, and to make them white, even to the time of the end: because it is yet for a time appointed. And the king shall do according to his will; and he shall exalt himself, and magnify himself above every god, and shall speak marvellous things against the God of gods, and shall prosper till the indignation be accomplished: for that that is determined shall be done. Neither shall he regard the God of his fathers, nor the desire of women, nor regard any god: for he shall magnify himself above all. But in his estate shall he honour the God of forces: and a god whom his fathers knew not shall he honour with gold, and silver, and with precious stones, and pleasant things.

"Thus shall he do in the most strong holds with a strange god, whom he shall acknowledge and increase with glory: and he shall cause them to rule over many, and shall divide the land for gain. And at the time of the end shall the king of the south push at him: and the king of the north shall come against him like a whirlwind, with chariots, and with horsemen, and with many ships; and he shall enter into the countries, and shall overflow and pass over. He shall enter also into the glorious land, and many countries shall be overthrown: but these shall escape out of his hand, even Edom, and Moab, and the chief of the children of Ammon. He shall stretch forth his hand also upon the countries: and the land of Egypt shall not escape. But he shall have power over the treasures of gold and of silver, and over all the precious things of Egypt: and the Libyans and the Ethiopians shall be at his steps. But tidings out of the east and out of the north shall trouble him: therefore he shall go forth with great fury to destroy, and utterly to make away many. And he shall plant the tabernacles of his palace between the seas in the glorious holy mountain; yet he shall come to his end, and none shall help him.

"And at that time shall Michael stand up, the great prince which standeth for the children of thy people: and there shall be a time of trouble, such as never was since there was a nation even to that same time: and at that time thy people shall be delivered, every one that shall be found written in the book. And many of them that sleep in the dust of the earth shall awake, some to everlasting life, and some to shame and everlasting contempt. And they that be wise shall shine as the brightness of the firmament; and they that turn many to righteousness as the stars for ever and ever.

"But thou, O Daniel, shut up the words, and seal the book, even to the time of the end: many shall run to and fro, and knowledge shall be increased."

Then I Daniel looked, and, behold, there stood other two, the one on this side of the bank of the river, and the other on that side of the bank of the river. And one said to the man clothed in linen, which was upon the waters of the river, "How long shall it be to the end of these wonders?" And I heard the man clothed in linen, which was upon the waters of the river, when he held up his right hand and his left hand unto heaven, and sware by him that liveth for ever that it shall be for a time, times, and an half; and when he shall have accomplished to scatter the power of the holy people, all these things shall be finished.

And I heard, but I understood not: then said I, "O my Lord, what shall be the end of these things?" And he said, "Go thy way, Daniel: for the words are closed up and sealed till the time of the end. Many shall be purified, and made white, and tried; but the wicked shall do wickedly: and none of the wicked shall understand; but the wise shall understand. And from the time that the daily sacrifice shall be taken away, and the abomination that maketh desolate set up, there shall be a thousand two hundred and ninety days. Blessed is he that waiteth, and cometh to the thousand three hundred and five and thirty days. But go thou thy way till the end be: for thou shalt rest, and stand in thy lot at the end of the days."

HOSEA

THE word of the Lord that came unto Hosea the son of Beeri, in the days of Uzziah, Jotham, Ahaz, and Hezekiah, kings of Judah, and in the days of Jeroboam the son of Joash, king of Israel.

THE beginning of the word of the Lord by Hosea.

And the Lord said to Hosea, "Go, take unto thee a wife of whoredoms and children of whoredoms: for the land hath committed great whoredom, departing from the Lord." So he went and took Gomer the daughter of Diblaim; which conceived, and bare him a son. And the Lord said unto him, "Call his name Jezreel; for yet a little while, and I will avenge the blood of Jezreel upon the house of Jehu, and will cause to cease the kingdom of the house of Israel. And it shall come to pass at that day, that I will break the bow of Israel in the valley of Jezreel."

And she conceived again, and bare a daughter. And God said unto him, "Call her name Lo-ruhamah: for I will no more have mercy upon the house of Israel; but I will utterly take them away. But I will have mercy upon the house of Judah, and will save them by the Lord their God, and will not save them by bow, nor by sword, nor by battle, by horses, nor by horsemen."

Now when she had weaned Lo-ruhamah, she conceived, and bare a son. Then said God, "Call his name Lo-ammi: for ye are not my people, and I will not be your God. Yet the number of the children of Israel shall be as the sand of the sea, which cannot be measured nor numbered; and it shall come to pass, that in the place where it was said unto them, Ye are not my people, there it shall be said unto them, Ye are the sons of the living God. Then shall the children of Judah and the children of Israel be gathered together, and appoint themselves one head, and they shall come up out of the land: for great shall be the day of Jezreel.

"Say ye unto your brethren, Ammi; and to your sisters, Ru-hamah. Plead with your mother, plead: for she is not my wife, neither am I her husband: let her therefore put away her whoredoms out of her sight, and her adulteries from between her breasts; lest I strip her naked, and set her as in the day that she was born, and make her as a wilderness, and set her like a dry land, and slay her with thirst. And I will not have mercy upon her children; for they be the children of whoredoms. For their mother hath played the harlot: she that conceived them hath done shamefully: for she said, I will go after my lovers, that give me my bread and my water, my wool and my flax, mine oil and my drink.

" Therefore, behold, I will hedge up thy way with thorns, and make a wall, that she shall not find her paths. And she shall follow after her lovers, but she shall not overtake them; and she shall seek them, but shall not find them: then shall she say, I will go and return to my first husband; for then was it better with me than now.

"For she did not know that I gave her corn, and wine, and oil, and multiplied her silver and gold, which they prepared for Baal. Therefore will I return, and take away my corn in the time thereof, and my wine in the season thereof, and will recover my wool and my flax given to cover her nakedness. And now will I discover her lewdness in the sight of her lovers, and none shall deliver her out of mine hand. I will also cause all her mirth to cease, her feast days, her new moons, and her sabbaths, and all her solemn feasts. And I will destroy her vines and her fig trees, whereof she hath said, These are my rewards that my lovers have given me: and I will make them a forest, and the beasts of the field shall eat them. And I will visit upon her the days of Baalim, wherein she burned incense to them, and she decked herself with her earrings and her jewels, and she went after her lovers, and forgat me, saith the Lord.

"Therefore, behold, I will allure her, and bring her into the wilderness, and speak comfortably unto her. And I will give her her vineyards from thence, and the valley of Achor for a door of hope: and she shall sing there, as in the days of her youth, and as in the day when she came up out of the land of Egypt. And it shall be at that day, saith the Lord, that thou shalt call me Ishi; and shalt call me no more Baali. For I will take away the names of Baalim out of her mouth, and they shall no more be remembered by their name.

"And in that day will I make a covenant for them with the beasts of the field, and with the fowls of heaven, and with the creeping things of the ground: and I will break the bow and the sword and the battle out of the earth, and will make them to lie down safely. And I will betroth thee unto me for ever; yea, I will betroth thee unto me in righteousness, and in judgment, and in lovingkindness, and in mercies. I will even betroth thee unto me in faithfulness: and thou shalt know the Lord. And it shall come to pass in that day, I will hear, saith the Lord, I will hear the heavens, and they shall hear the earth; and the earth shall hear the corn, and the wine, and the oil; and they shall hear Jezreel. And I will sow her unto me in the earth; and I will have mercy upon her that had not obtained mercy; and I will say to them which were not my people, Thou art my people; and they shall say, Thou art my God."

Then said the Lord unto me, "Go yet, love a woman beloved of her friend, yet an adulteress, according to the love of the Lord toward the children of Israel, who look to other gods, and love flagons of wine." So I bought her to me for fifteen pieces of silver, and for an homer of barley, and an half homer of barley. And I said unto her, "Thou shalt abide for me many days; thou shalt not play the harlot, and thou shalt not be for another man: so will I also be for thee."

For the children of Israel shall abide many days without a king, and without a prince, and without a sacrifice, and without an image, and without an ephod, and without teraphim: afterward shall the children of Israel return, and seek the Lord their God, and David their king; and shall fear the Lord and his goodness in the latter days.

Hear the word of the Lord, ye children of Israel: for the Lord hath a controversy with the inhabitants of the land, because there is no truth, nor mercy, nor knowledge of God in the land. By swearing, and lying, and killing, and stealing, and committing adultery, they break out, and blood toucheth blood. Therefore shall the land mourn, and every one that dwelleth therein shall languish, with the beasts of the field, and with the fowls of heaven; yea, the fishes of the sea also shall be taken away.

Yet let no man strive, nor reprove another: for thy people are as they that strive with the priest. Therefore shalt thou fall in the day, and the prophet also shall fall with thee in the night, and I will destroy thy mother. My people are destroyed for lack of knowledge: because thou hast rejected knowledge, I will also reject thee, that thou shalt be no priest to me: seeing thou hast forgotten the law of thy God, I will also forget thy children. As they were increased, so they sinned against me: therefore will I change their glory into shame. They eat up the sin of my people, and they set their heart on their iniquity. And there shall be, like people, like priest: and I will punish them for their ways, and reward them their doings. For they shall eat, and not have enough: they shall commit whoredom, and shall not increase: because they have left off to take heed to the Lord.

Whoredom and wine and new wine take away the heart. My people ask counsel at their stocks, and their staff declareth unto them: for the spirit of whoredoms hath caused them to err, and they have gone a whoring from under their God. They sacrifice upon the tops of the mountains, and burn incense upon the hills, under oaks and poplars and elms, because the shadow thereof is good: therefore your daughters shall commit whoredom, and your spouses shall commit adultery. I will not punish your daughters when they commit whoredom, nor your spouses when they commit adultery: for themselves are separated with whores, and they sacrifice with harlots: therefore the people that doth not understand shall fall.

Though thou, Israel, play the harlot, yet let not Judah offend; and come not ye unto Gilgal, neither go ye up to Beth-aven, nor swear, "The Lord liveth." For Israel slideth back as a backsliding heifer: now the Lord will feed them as a lamb in a large place.

Ephraim is joined to idols: let him alone. Their drink is sour: they have committed whoredom continually: her rulers with shame do love Give ye. The wind hath bound her up in her wings, and they shall be ashamed because of their sacrifices. Hear ye this, O priests; and hearken, ye house of Israel; and give ye ear, O house of the king; for judgment is toward you, because ye have been a snare on Mizpah, and a net spread upon Tabor. And the revolters are profound to make slaughter, though I have been a rebuker of them all.

I know Ephraim, and Israel is not hid from me: for now, O Ephraim, thou committest whoredom, and Israel is defiled. They will not frame their doings to turn unto their God: for the spirit of whoredoms is in the midst of them, and they have not known the Lord. And the pride of Israel doth testify to his face: therefore shall Israel and Ephraim fall in their iniquity; Judah also shall fall with them. They shall go with their flocks and with their herds to seek the Lord; but they shall not find him; he hath withdrawn himself from them. They have dealt treacherously against the Lord: for they have begotten strange children: now shall a month devour them with their portions.

Blow ye the cornet in Gibeah, and the trumpet in Ramah: cry aloud at Beth-aven, after thee, O Benjamin. Ephraim shall be desolate in the day of rebuke: among the tribes of Israel have I made known that which shall surely be. The princes of Judah were like them that remove the bound: therefore I will pour out my wrath upon them like water. Ephraim is oppressed and broken in judgment, because he willingly walked after the commandment. Therefore will I be unto Ephraim as a moth, and to the house of Judah as rottenness.

When Ephraim saw his sickness, and Judah saw his wound, then went Ephraim to the Assyrian, and sent to king Jareb: yet could he not heal you, nor cure you of your wound. For I will be unto Ephraim as a lion, and as a young lion to the house of Judah: I, even I, will tear and go away; I will take away, and none shall rescue him. I will go and return to my place, till they acknowledge their offence, and seek my face: in their affliction they will seek me early.

Come, and let us return unto the Lord: for he hath torn, and he will heal us; he hath smitten, and he will bind us up. After two days will he revive us: in the third day he will raise us up, and we shall live in his sight. Then shall we know, if we follow on to know the Lord: his going forth is prepared as the morning; and he shall come unto us as the rain, as the latter and former rain unto the earth.

O Ephraim, what shall I do unto thee? O Judah, what shall I do unto thee? for your goodness is as a morning cloud, and as the early dew it goeth away. Therefore have I hewed them by the prophets; I have slain them by the words of my mouth: and thy judgments are as the light that goeth forth. For I desired mercy, and not sacrifice; and the knowledge of God more than burnt offerings. But they like men have transgressed the covenant: there have they dealt treacherously against me. Gilead is a city of them that work iniquity, and is polluted with blood. And as troops of robbers wait for a man, so the company of priests murder in the way by consent: for they commit lewdness.

I have seen an horrible thing in the house of Israel: there is the whoredom of Ephraim, Israel is defiled. Also, O Judah, he hath set an harvest for thee, when I returned the captivity of my people. When I would have healed Israel, then the iniquity of Ephraim was discovered, and the wickedness of Samaria: for they commit falsehood; and the thief cometh in, and the troop of robbers spoileth without. And they consider not in their hearts that I remember all their wickedness: now their own doings have beset them about; they are before my face.

They make the king glad with their wickedness, and the princes with their lies. They are all adulterers, as an oven heated by the baker, who ceaseth from raising after he hath kneaded the dough, until it be leavened. In the day of our king the princes have made him sick with bottles of wine; he stretched out his hand with scorners. For they have made ready their heart like an oven, whiles they lie in wait: their baker sleepeth all the night; in the morning it burneth as a flaming fire. They are all hot as an oven, and have devoured their judges; all their kings are fallen: there is none among them that calleth unto me.

Ephraim, he hath mixed himself among the people; Ephraim is a cake not turned. Strangers have devoured his strength, and he knoweth it not: yea, gray hairs are here and there upon him, yet he knoweth not. And the pride of Israel testifieth to his face: and they do not return to the Lord their God, nor seek him for all this.

Ephraim also is like a silly dove without heart: they call to Egypt, they go to Assyria. When they shall go, I will spread my net upon them; I will bring them down as the fowls of the heaven; I will chastise them, as their congregation hath heard. Woe unto them! for they have fled from me: destruction unto them! because they have transgressed against me: though I have redeemed them, yet they have spoken lies against me. And they have not cried unto me with their heart, when they howled upon their beds: they assemble themselves for corn and wine, and they rebel against me. Though I have bound and strengthened their arms, yet do they imagine mischief against me. They return, but not to the Most High: they are like a deceitful bow: their princes shall fall by the sword for the rage of their tongue: this shall be their derision in the land of Egypt.

Set the trumpet to thy mouth. He shall come as an eagle against the house of the Lord, because they have transgressed my covenant, and trespassed against my law.

Israel shall cry unto me, "My God, we know

thee." Israel hath cast off the thing that is good: the enemy shall pursue him. They have set up kings, but not by me: they have made princes, and I knew it not: of their silver and their gold have they made them idols, that they may be cut off. Thy calf, O Samaria, hath cast thee off; mine anger is kindled against them: how long will it be ere they attain to innocency? for from Israel was it also: the workman made it; therefore it is not God: but the calf of Samaria shall be broken in pieces. For they have sown the wind, and they shall reap the whirlwind: it hath no stalk: the bud shall yield no meal: if so be it yield, the strangers shall swallow it up.

Israel is swallowed up: now shall they be among the Gentiles as a vessel wherein is no pleasure. For they are gone up to Assyria, a wild ass alone by himself: Ephraim hath hired lovers. Yea, though they have hired among the nations, now will I gather them, and they shall sorrow a little for the burden of the king of princes. Because Ephraim hath made many altars to sin, altars shall be unto him to sin. I have written to him the great things of my law, but they were counted as a strange thing. They sacrifice flesh for the sacrifices of mine offerings, and eat it; but the Lord accepteth them not; now will he remember their iniquity, and visit their sins: they shall return to Egypt. For

Israel hath forgotten his Maker, and buildeth temples; and Judah hath multiplied fenced cities: but I will send a fire upon his cities, and it shall devour the palaces thereof.

Rejoice not, O Israel, for joy, as other people: for thou hast gone a whoring from thy God, thou hast loved a reward upon every cornfloor. The floor and the winepress shall not feed them, and the new wine shall fail in her. They shall not dwell in the Lord's land; but Ephraim shall return to Egypt, and they shall eat unclean things in Assyria. They shall not offer wine offerings to the Lord, neither shall they be pleasing unto him: their sacrifices shall be unto them as the bread of mourners; all that eat thereof shall be polluted: for their bread for their soul shall not come into the house of the Lord. What will ye do in the solemn day, and in the day of the feast of the Lord? For, lo, they are gone because of destruction: Egypt shall gather them up, Memphis shall bury them: the pleasant places for their silver, nettles shall possess them: thorns shall be in their tabernacles.

The days of visitation are come, the days of recompence are come; Israel shall know it: the prophet is a fool, the spiritual man is mad, for the multitude of thine iniquity, and the great hatred. The watchman of Ephraim was with my God: but the prophet is a snare of a fowler in all his ways, and hatred in the house of his God. They have deeply corrupted themselves, as in the days of Gibeah: therefore he will remember their iniquity, he will visit their sins. I found Israel like grapes in the wilderness; I saw your fathers as the first-ripe in the fig tree at her first time: but they went to Baal-peor, and separated themselves unto that shame; and their abominations were according as they loved.

As for Ephraim, their glory shall fly away like a bird, from the birth, and from the womb, and from the conception. Though they bring up their children, yet will I bereave them, that there shall not be a man left: yea, woe also to them when I depart from them! Ephraim, as I saw Tyrus, is planted in a pleasant place: but Ephraim shall bring forth his children to the murderer. Give them, O Lord: what wilt thou give? give them a miscarrying womb and dry breasts.

All their wickedness is in Gilgal: for there I hated them: for the wickedness of their doings I will drive them out of mine house, I will love them no more: all their princes are revolters. Ephraim is smitten, their root is dried up, they shall bear no fruit: yea, though they bring forth, yet will I slay even the beloved fruit of their womb. My God will cast them away, because they did not hearken unto him: and they shall be wanderers among the nations.

Israel is an empty vine, he bringeth forth fruit unto himself: according to the multitude of his fruit he hath increased the altars; according to the goodness of his land they have made goodly images. Their heart is divided; now shall they be found faulty: he shall break down their altars, he shall spoil their images. For now they shall say, "We have no king, because we feared not the Lord; what then should a king do to us?" They have spoken words, swearing falsely in making a covenant: thus judgment springeth up as hemlock in the furrows of the field.

The inhabitants of Samaria shall fear because of the calves of Beth-aven: for the people thereof shall mourn over it, and the priests thereof that rejoiced on it, for the glory thereof, because it is departed from it. It shall be also carried unto Assyria for a present to king Jareb: Ephraim shall receive shame, and Israel shall be ashamed of his own counsel. As for Samaria, her king is cut off as the foam upon the water. The high places also of Aven, the sin of Israel, shall be destroyed: the thorn and the thistle shall come up on their altars; and they shall say to the mountains, "Cover us;" and to the hills, " Fall on us."

O Israel, thou hast sinned from the days of Gibeah: there they stood: the battle in Gibeah against the children of iniquity did not overtake them. It is in my desire that I should chastise them; and the people shall be gathered against them, when they shall bind themselves in their two furrows. And Ephraim is as an heifer that is taught, and loveth to tread out the corn; but I passed over upon her fair neck: I will make Ephraim to ride; Judah shall plow, and Jacob shall break his clods. Sow to yourselves in righteousness, reap in mercy; break up your fallow ground: for it is time to seek the Lord, till he come and rain righteousness upon you.

Ye have plowed wickedness, ye have reaped iniquity; ye have eaten the fruit of lies: because thou didst trust in thy way, in the multitude of thy mighty men. Therefore shall a tumult arise among thy people, and all thy fortresses shall be spoiled, as Shalman spoiled Beth-arbel in the day of battle: the mother was dashed in pieces upon her children. So shall Beth-el do unto you because of your great wickedness: in a morning shall the king of Israel utterly be cut off.

When Israel was a child, then I loved him, and called my son out of Egypt. As they called them, so they went from them: they sacrificed unto Baalim, and burned incense to graven images. I taught Ephraim also to go, taking them by their arms; but they knew not that I healed them. I drew them with cords of a man, with bands of love: and I was to them as they that take off the yoke on their jaws, and I laid meat unto them. He shall not return into the land of Egypt, but the Assyrian shall be his king, because they refused to return. And the sword shall abide on his cities, and shall consume his branches, and devour them, because of their own counsels. And my people are bent to backsliding from me: though they called them to the Most High, none at all would exalt him.

How shall I give thee up, Ephraim? how shall I deliver thee, Israel? how shall I make thee as Admah? how shall I set thee as Zeboim? mine heart is turned within me, my repentings are kindled together. I will not execute the fierceness of mine anger, I will not return to destroy Ephraim: for I am God, and not man; the Holy One in the midst of thee: and I will not enter into the city. They shall walk after the Lord: he shall roar like a lion: when he shall roar, then the children shall tremble from the west. They shall tremble as a bird out of Egypt, and as a dove out of the land of Assyria: and I will place them in their houses, saith the Lord.

Ephraim compasseth me about with lies, and the house of Israel with deceit: but Judah yet ruleth with God, and is faithful with the saints.

Ephraim feedeth on wind, and followeth after the east wind: he daily increaseth lies and desolation; and they do make a covenant with the Assyrians, and oil is carried into Egypt.

The Lord hath also a controversy with Judah, and will punish Jacob according to his ways; according to his doings will he recompense him.

He took his brother by the heel in the womb, and by his strength he had power with God: yea, he had power over the Angel, and prevailed: he wept, and made supplication unto him: he found him in Beth-el, and there he spake with us; even the Lord God of Hosts; the Lord is his memorial. Therefore turn thou to thy God: keep mercy and judgment, and wait on thy God continually.

He is a merchant, the balances of deceit are in his hand: he loveth to oppress. And Ephraim said, "Yet I am become rich, I have found me out substance: in all my labours they shall find none iniquity in me that were sin."

And I that am the Lord thy God from the land of Egypt will yet make thee to dwell in tabernacles, as in the days of the solemn feast. I have also spoken by the prophets, and I have multiplied visions, and used similitudes, by the ministry of the prophets.

Is there iniquity in Gilead? surely they are vanity: they sacrifice bullocks in Gilgal; yea, their altars are as heaps in the furrows of the fields. (And Jacob fled into the country of Syria, and Israel served for a wife, and for a wife he kept sheep. And by a prophet the Lord brought Israel out of Egypt, and by a prophet was he preserved.) Ephraim provoked him to anger most bitterly: therefore shall he leave his blood upon him, and his reproach shall his Lord return unto him.

When Ephraim spake trembling, he exalted himself in Israel; but when he offended in Baal, he died. And now they sin more and more, and have made them molten images of their silver, and idols according to their own understanding, all of it the work of the craftsmen: they say of them, "Let the men that sacrifice kiss the calves." Therefore they shall be as the morning cloud, and as the early dew that passeth away, as the chaff that is driven with the whirlwind out of the floor, and as the smoke out of the chimney.

Yet I am the Lord thy God from the land of Egypt, and thou shalt know no god but me: for there is no saviour beside me. I did know thee in the wilderness, in the land of great drought.

According to their pasture, so were they filled; they were filled, and their heart was exalted; therefore have they forgotten me. Therefore I will be unto them as a lion: as a leopard by the way will I observe them: I will meet them as a bear that is bereaved of her whelps, and will rend the caul of their heart, and there will I devour them like a lion: the wild beast shall tear them.

O Israel, thou hast destroyed thyself; but in

me is thine help. I will be thy king: where is any other that may save thee in all thy cities? and thy judges of whom thou saidst, "Give me a king and princes?" I gave thee a king in mine anger, and took him away in my wrath.

The iniquity of Ephraim is bound up; his sin is hid. The sorrows of a travailing woman shall come upon him: he is an unwise son; for he should not stay long in the place of the breaking forth of children. (I will ransom them from the power of the grave; I will redeem them from death: O death, I will be thy plagues; O grave, I will be thy destruction!) Repentance shall be hid from mine eyes. Though he be fruitful among his brethren, an east wind shall come, the wind of the Lord shall come up from the wilderness, and his spring shall become dry, and his fountain shall be dried up: he shall spoil the treasure of all pleasant vessels. Samaria shall become desolate; for she hath rebelled against her God: they shall fall by the sword: their infants shall be dashed in pieces, and their women with child shall be ripped up.

O Israel, return unto the Lord thy God; for thou hast fallen by thine iniquity. Take with you words, and turn to the Lord: say unto him, "Take away all iniquity, and receive us graciously: so will we render the calves of our lips. Asshur shall not save us; we will not ride upon horses: neither will we say any more to the work of our hands, Ye are our gods: for in thee the fatherless findeth mercy."

I will heal their backsliding, I will love them freely: for mine anger is turned away from him. I will be as the dew unto Israel: he shall grow as the lily, and cast forth his roots as Lebanon. His branches shall spread, and his beauty shall be as the olive tree, and his smell as Lebanon. They that dwell under his shadow shall return; they shall revive as the corn, and grow as the vine; the scent thereof shall be as the wine of Lebanon. Ephraim shall say, "What have I to do any more with idols?" I have heard him, and observed him: I am like a green fir tree. From me is thy fruit found.

Who is wise, and he shall understand these things? prudent, and he shall know them? for the ways of the Lord are right, and the just shall walk in them: but the transgressors shall fall therein.

JOEL

THE word of the Lord that came to Joel the son of Pethuel.

HEAR this, ye old men, and give ear, all ye inhabitants of the land. Hath this been in your days, or even in the days of your fathers? Tell ye your children of it, and let your children tell their children, and their children another generation. That which the palmerworm hath left hath the locust eaten; and that which the locust hath left hath the cankerworm eaten; and that which the cankerworm hath left hath the caterpiller eaten.

Awake, ye drunkards, and weep; and howl, all ye drinkers of wine, because of the new wine; for it is cut off from your mouth. For a nation is come up upon my land, strong, and without number, whose teeth are the teeth of a lion, and he hath the cheek teeth of a great lion. He hath laid my vine waste, and barked my fig tree: he hath made it clean bare, and cast it away; the branches thereof are made white.

Lament like a virgin girded with sackcloth for the husband of her youth. The meat offering and the drink offering is cut off from the house of the Lord; the priests, the Lord's ministers, mourn.

The field is wasted, the land mourneth; for the corn is wasted: the new wine is dried up, the oil languisheth. Be ye ashamed, O ye husbandmen; howl, O ye vinedressers, for the wheat and for the barley; because the harvest of the field is perished. The vine is dried up, and the fig tree languisheth; the pomegranate tree, the palm tree also, and the apple tree, even all the trees of the field, are withered: because joy is withered away from the sons of men.

Gird yourselves, and lament, ye priests: howl, ye ministers of the altar: come, lie all night in sackcloth, ye ministers of my God: for the meat offering and the drink offering is withholden from the house of your God. Sanctify ye a fast, call a solemn assembly, gather the elders and all the inhabitants of the land into the house of the Lord your God, and cry unto the Lord, "Alas for the day!" for the day of the Lord is at hand, and as a destruction from the Almighty shall it come.

Is not the meat cut off before our eyes, yea, joy and gladness from the house of our God? The seed is rotten under their clods, the garners are laid desolate, the barns are broken down; for the corn is withered. How do the beasts groan! the herds of cattle are perplexed, because they have no pasture; yea, the flocks of sheep are made desolate. O Lord, to thee will I cry: for the fire hath devoured the pastures of the wilderness, and the flame hath burned all the trees of the field. The beasts of the field cry also unto thee: for the rivers of waters are dried up, and the fire hath devoured the pastures of the wilderness.

Blow ye the trumpet in Zion, and sound an alarm in my holy mountain: let all the inhabitants of the land tremble: for the day of the Lord cometh, for it is nigh at hand; a day of darkness and of gloominess, a day of clouds and of thick darkness, as the morning spread upon the mountains: a great people and a strong; there hath not been ever the like, neither shall be any more after it, even to the years of many generations.

A fire devoureth before them; and behind them a flame burneth: the land is as the garden of Eden before them, and behind them a desolate wilderness; yea, and nothing shall escape them. The appearance of them is as the appearance of horses; and as horsemen, so shall they run. Like the noise of chariots on the tops of mountains shall they leap, like the noise of a flame of fire that devoureth the stubble, as a strong people set in battle array. Before their face the people shall be much pained: all faces shall gather blackness. They shall run like mighty men; they shall climb the wall like men of war; and they shall march every one on his ways, and they shall not break their ranks: neither shall one thrust another; they shall walk every one in his path: and when they fall upon the sword, they shall not be wounded. They shall run to and fro in the city; they shall run upon the wall, they shall climb up upon the houses; they shall enter in at the windows like a thief. The earth shall quake before them; the heavens shall tremble: the sun and the moon shall be dark, and the stars shall withdraw their shining: and the Lord shall utter his voice before his army: for his camp is very great: for he is strong that executeth his word: for the day of the Lord is great and very terrible; and who can abide it?

Therefore also now, saith the Lord, turn ye even to me with all your heart, and with fasting, and with weeping, and with mourning: and rend your heart, and not your garments, and turn unto the Lord your God: for he is gracious and merciful, slow to anger, and of great kindness, and repenteth him of the evil. Who knoweth if he will return and repent, and leave a blessing behind him? even a meat offering and a drink offering unto the Lord your God.

Blow the trumpet in Zion, sanctify a fast,

call a solemn assembly: gather the people, sanctify the congregation, assemble the elders, gather the children, and those that suck the breasts: let the bridegroom go forth of his chamber, and the bride out of her closet. Let the priests, the ministers of the Lord, weep between the porch and the altar, and let them say, " Spare thy people, O Lord, and give not thine heritage to reproach, that the heathen should rule over them: wherefore should they say among the people, Where is their God?" Then will the Lord be jealous for his land, and pity his people. Yea, the Lord will answer and say unto his people, "Behold, I will send you corn, and wine, and oil, and ye shall be satisfied therewith: and I will no more make you a reproach among the heathen: but I will remove far off from you the northern army, and will drive him into a land barren and desolate, with his face toward the east sea, and his hinder part toward the utmost sea, and his stink shall come up, and his ill savour shall come up, because he hath done great things."

Fear not, O land; be glad and rejoice: for the Lord will do great things. Be not afraid, ye beasts of the field: for the pastures of the wilderness do spring, for the tree beareth her fruit, the fig tree and the vine do yield their strength. Be glad then, ye children of Zion, and rejoice in the Lord your God: for he hath given you the former rain moderately, and he will cause to come down for you the rain, the former rain, and the latter rain, in the first month. And the floors shall be full of wheat, and the fats shall overflow with wine and oil. And I will restore to you the years that the locust hath eaten, the cankerworm, and the caterpiller, and the palmerworm, my great army which I sent among you. And ye shall eat in plenty, and be satisfied, and praise the name of the Lord your God, that hath dealt wondrously with you: and my people shall never be ashamed. And ye shall know that I am in the midst of Israel, and that I am the Lord your God, and none else: and my people shall never be ashamed.

And it shall come to pass afterward, that I will pour out my spirit upon all flesh; and your sons and your daughters shall prophesy, your old men shall dream dreams, your young men shall see visions: and also upon the servants and upon the handmaids in those days will I pour out my spirit. And I will shew wonders in the heavens and in the earth, blood, and fire, and pillars of smoke. The sun shall be turned into darkness, and the moon into blood, before the great and the terrible day of the Lord come.

And it shall come to pass, that whosoever shall call on the name of the Lord shall be delivered: for in mount Zion and in Jerusalem shall be deliverance, as the Lord hath said, and in the remnant whom the Lord shall call. For, behold, in those days, and in that time, when I shall bring again the captivity of Judah and Jerusalem, I will also gather all nations, and will bring them down into the valley of Jehoshaphat, and will plead with them there for my people and for my heritage Israel, whom they have scattered among the nations, and parted my land: and they have cast lots for my people ; and have given a boy for an harlot, and sold a girl for wine, that they might drink.

Yea, and what have ye to do with me, O Tyre, and Zidon, and all the coasts of Palestine? will ye render me a recompence? and if ye recompense me, swiftly and speedily will I return your recompence upon your own head; because ye have taken my silver and my gold, and have carried into your temples my goodly pleasant things: the children also of Judah and the children of Jerusalem have ye sold unto the Grecians, that ye might remove them far from their border. Behold, I will raise them out of the place whither ye have sold them, and will return your recompence upon your own head: and I will sell your sons and your daughters into the hand of the children of Judah, and they shall sell them to the Sabeans, to a people far off: for the Lord hath spoken it.

Proclaim ye this among the Gentiles; Prepare war, wake up the mighty men, let all the men of war draw near; let them come up: beat your plowshares into swords, and your pruninghooks into spears: let the weak say, "I am strong." Assemble yourselves, and come, all ye heathen, and gather yourselves together round about: thither cause thy mighty ones to come down, O Lord.

Let the heathen be wakened, and come up to the valley of Jehoshaphat: for there will I sit to judge all the heathen round about. Put ye in the sickle, for the harvest is ripe: come, get you down; for the press is full, the fats overflow; for their wickedness is great. Multitudes, multitudes in the valley of decision: for the day of the Lord is near in the valley of decision. The sun and the moon shall be darkened, and the stars shall withdraw their shining. The Lord also shall roar out of Zion, and utter his voice from Jerusalem; and the heavens and the earth shall shake: but the Lord will be the hope of his people, and the strength of the children of Israel. So shall ye know that I am the Lord your God dwelling in Zion, my holy mountain: then shall Jerusalem be holy, and there shall no strangers pass through her any more.

And it shall come to pass in that day, that the mountains shall drop down new wine, and the hills shall flow with milk, and all the rivers of Judah shall flow with waters, and a fountain shall come forth of the house of the Lord, and shall water the valley of Shittim. Egypt shall be a desolation, and Edom shall be a desolate wilderness, for the violence against the children of Judah, because they have shed innocent blood in their land. But Judah shall dwell for ever, and Jerusalem from generation to generation. For I will cleanse their blood that I have not cleansed: for the Lord dwelleth in Zion.

AMOS

THE words of Amos, who was among the herdmen of Tekoa, which he saw concerning Israel in the days of Uzziah king of Judah, and in the days of Jeroboam the son of Joash king of Israel, two years before the earthquake. And he said,

THE Lord will roar from Zion, and utter his voice from Jerusalem; and the habitations of the shepherds shall mourn, and the top of Carmel shall wither.

Thus saith the Lord; For three transgressions of Damascus, and for four, I will not turn away the punishment thereof; because they have threshed Gilead with threshing instruments of iron: but I will send a fire into the house of Hazael, which shall devour the palaces of Benhadad. I will break also the bar of Damascus, and cut off the inhabitant from the plain of Aven, and him that holdeth the sceptre from the house of Eden: and the people of Syria shall go into captivity unto Kir, saith the Lord.

Thus saith the Lord; For three transgressions of Gaza, and for four, I will not turn away the punishment thereof; because they carried away captive the whole captivity, to deliver them up to Edom: but I will send a fire on the wall of Gaza, which shall devour the palaces thereof: and I will cut off the inhabitant from Ashdod, and him that holdeth the sceptre from Ashkelon, and I will turn mine hand against Ekron: and the remnant of the Philistines shall perish, saith the Lord God.

Thus saith the Lord; For three transgressions of Tyrus, and for four, I will not turn away the punishment thereof; because they delivered up the whole captivity to Edom, and remembered not the brotherly covenant: but I will send a fire on the wall of Tyrus, which shall devour the palaces thereof.

Thus saith the Lord; For three transgressions of Edom, and for four, I will not turn away the punishment thereof; because he did pursue his brother with the sword, and did cast off all pity, and his anger did tear perpetually, and he kept his wrath for ever: but I will send a fire upon Teman, which shall devour the palaces of Bozrah.

Thus saith the Lord; For three transgressions of the children of Ammon, and for four, I will not turn away the punishment thereof; because they have ripped up the women with child of Gilead, that they might enlarge their border: but I will kindle a fire in the wall of Rabbah, and it shall devour the palaces thereof, with shouting in the day of battle, with a tempest in the day of the whirlwind: and their king shall go into captivity, he and his princes together, saith the Lord.

Thus saith the Lord; For three transgressions of Moab, and for four, I will not turn away the punishment thereof; because he burned the bones of the king of Edom into lime: but I will send a fire upon Moab, and it shall devour the palaces of Kirioth: and Moab shall die with tumult, with shouting, and with the sound of the trumpet: and I will cut off the judge from the midst thereof, and will slay all the princes thereof with him, saith the Lord.

Thus saith the Lord; For three transgressions of Judah, and for four, I will not turn away the punishment thereof; because they have despised the law of the Lord, and have not kept his commandments, and their lies caused them to err, after the which their fathers have walked: but I will send a fire upon Judah, and it shall devour the palaces of Jerusalem.

Thus saith the Lord; For three transgressions of Israel, and for four, I will not turn away the punishment thereof; because they sold the righteous for silver, and the poor for a pair of shoes; that pant after the dust of the earth on the head of the poor, and turn aside the way of the meek: and a man and his father will go in unto the same maid, to profane my holy name: and they lay themselves down upon clothes laid to pledge by every altar, and they drink the wine of the condemned in the house of their god.

Yet destroyed I the Amorite before them, whose height was like the height of the cedars, and he was strong as the oaks; yet I destroyed his fruit from above, and his roots from beneath. Also I brought you up from the land of Egypt, and led you forty years through the wilderness, to possess the land of the Amorite. And I raised up of your sons for prophets, and of your young men for Nazarites. Is it not even thus, O ye children of Israel? saith the Lord. But ye gave the Nazarites wine to drink; and commanded the prophets, saying, "Prophesy not."

Behold, I am pressed under you, as a cart is pressed that is full of sheaves. Therefore the flight shall perish from the swift, and the strong shall not strengthen his force, neither shall the mighty deliver himself: neither shall he stand that handleth the bow; and he that is swift of foot shall not deliver himself: neither shall he that rideth the horse deliver himself. And he that is courageous among the mighty shall flee away naked in that day, saith the Lord.

Hear this word that the Lord hath spoken against you, O children of Israel, against the whole family which I brought up from the land of Egypt, saying, "You only have I known of all the families of the earth: therefore I will punish you for all your iniquities."

Can two walk together, except they be agreed? will a lion roar in the forest, when he hath no prey? will a young lion cry out of his den, if he have taken nothing? can a bird fall in a snare upon the earth, where no gin is for him? shall one take up a snare from the earth, and have taken nothing at all? shall a trumpet be blown in the city, and the people not be afraid? shall there be evil in a city, and the Lord hath not done it?

Surely the Lord God will do nothing, but he revealeth his secret unto his servants the prophets. The lion hath roared, who will not fear? the Lord God hath spoken, who can but prophesy?

Publish in the palaces at Ashdod, and in the palaces in the land of Egypt, and say, "Assemble yourselves upon the mountains of Samaria, and behold the great tumults in the midst thereof, and the oppressed in the midst thereof." For they know not to do right, saith the Lord, who store up violence and robbery in their palaces. Therefore thus saith the Lord God; An adversary there shall be even round about the land; and he shall bring down thy strength from thee, and thy palaces shall be spoiled. Thus saith the Lord; As the shepherd taketh out of the mouth of the lion two legs, or a piece of an ear; so shall the children of Israel be taken out that dwell in Samaria in the corner of a bed, and in Damascus in a couch.

Hear ye, and testify in the house of Jacob, saith the Lord God, the God of Hosts, that in the day that I shall visit the transgressions of Israel upon him I will also visit the altars of Beth-el: and the horns of the altar shall be cut off, and fall to the ground. And I will smite the winter house with the summer house; and the houses of ivory shall perish, and the great houses shall have an end, saith the Lord.

Hear this word, ye kine of Bashan, that are in the mountain of Samaria, which oppress the poor, which crush the needy, which say to their masters, "Bring, and let us drink." The Lord God hath sworn by his holiness, that, lo, the days shall come upon you, that he will take you away with hooks, and your posterity with fishhooks. And ye shall go out at the breaches, every cow at that which is before her; and ye shall cast them into the palace, saith the Lord.

Come to Beth-el, and transgress; at Gilgal multiply transgression; and bring your sacrifices every morning, and your tithes after three years: and offer a sacrifice of thanksgiving with leaven, and proclaim and publish the free offerings: for this liketh you, O ye children of Israel, saith the Lord God.

And I also have given you cleanness of teeth in all your cities, and want of bread in all your places: yet have ye not returned unto me, saith the Lord.

And also I have withholden the rain from you, when there were yet three months to the harvest: and I caused it to rain upon one city, and caused it not to rain upon another city: one piece was rained upon, and the piece whereupon it rained not withered. So two or three cities wandered unto one city, to drink water; but they were not satisfied: yet have ye not returned unto me, saith the Lord.

I have smitten you with blasting and mildew: when your gardens and your vineyards and your fig trees and your olive trees increased, the palmerworm devoured them: yet have ye not returned unto me, saith the Lord.

I have sent among you the pestilence after the manner of Egypt: your young men have I slain with the sword, and have taken away your horses; and I have made the stink of your camps to come up unto your nostrils: yet have ye not returned unto me, saith the Lord.

I have overthrown some of you, as God overthrew Sodom and Gomorrah, and ye were as a firebrand plucked out of the burning: yet have ye not returned unto me, saith the Lord.

Therefore thus will I do unto thee, O Israel: and because I will do this unto thee, prepare to meet thy God, O Israel. For, lo, he that formeth the mountains, and createth the wind, and declareth unto man what is his thought, that maketh the morning darkness, and treadeth upon the high places of the earth, The Lord, The God of Hosts, is his name.

Hear ye this word which I take up against you, even a lamentation, O house of Israel. The virgin of Israel is fallen; she shall no more rise: she is forsaken upon her land; there is none to raise her up. For thus saith the Lord God; The city that went out by a thousand shall leave an hundred, and that which went forth by an hundred shall leave ten, to the house of Israel.

For thus saith the Lord unto the house of Israel, Seek ye me, and ye shall live: but seek not Beth-el, nor enter into Gilgal, and pass not to Beer-sheba: for Gilgal shall surely go into captivity, and Beth-el shall come to nought. Seek the Lord, and ye shall live; lest he break out like fire in the house of Joseph, and devour it, and there be none to quench it in Beth-el. Ye who turn judgment to wormwood, and leave off righteousness in the earth, seek him that maketh the seven stars and Orion, and turneth the shadow of death into the morning, and maketh the day dark with night: that calleth for the waters of the sea, and poureth them out upon the face of the earth: The Lord is his name: that strengtheneth the spoiled against the strong, so that the spoiled shall come against the fortress.

They hate him that rebuketh in the gate,

and they abhor him that speaketh uprightly. Forasmuch therefore as your treading is upon the poor, and ye take from him burdens of wheat: ye have built houses of hewn stone, but ye shall not dwell in them; ye have planted pleasant vineyards, but ye shall not drink wine of them. For I know your manifold transgressions and your mighty sins: they afflict the just, they take a bribe, and they turn aside the poor in the gate from their right. Therefore the prudent shall keep silence in that time; for it is an evil time.

Seek good, and not evil, that ye may live: and so the Lord, the God of Hosts, shall be with you, as ye have spoken. Hate the evil, and love the good, and establish judgment in the gate: it may be that the Lord God of Hosts will be gracious unto the remnant of Joseph.

Therefore the Lord, the God of Hosts, the Lord, saith thus; Wailing shall be in all streets; and they shall say in all the highways, "Alas! alas!" and they shall call the husbandman to mourning, and such as are skilful of lamentation to wailing. And in all vineyards shall be wailing: for I will pass through thee, saith the Lord.

Woe unto you that desire the day of the Lord! to what end is it for you? the day of the Lord is darkness, and not light. As if a man did flee from a lion, and a bear met him; or went into the house, and leaned his hand on the wall, and a serpent bit him. Shall not the day of the Lord be darkness, and not light? even very dark, and no brightness in it?

I hate, I despise your feast days, and I will not smell in your solemn assemblies. Though ye offer me burnt offerings and your meat offerings, I will not accept them: neither will I regard the peace offerings of your fat beasts. Take thou away from me the noise of thy songs; for I will not hear the melody of thy viols. But let judgment run down as waters, and righteousness as a mighty stream.

Have ye offered unto me sacrifices and offerings in the wilderness forty years, O house of Israel? but ye have borne the tabernacle of your Moloch and Chiun your images, the star of your god, which ye made to yourselves. Therefore will I cause you to go into captivity beyond Damascus, saith the Lord, whose name is the God of Hosts.

Woe to them that are at ease in Zion, and trust in the mountain of Samaria, which are named chief of the nations, to whom the house of Israel came! Pass ye unto Calneh, and see; and from thence go ye to Hamath the great: then go down to Gath of the Philistines: be they better than these kingdoms? or their border greater than your border, ye that put far away the evil day, and cause the seat of violence to come near? that lie upon beds of ivory, and stretch themselves upon their couches, and eat the lambs out of the flock, and the calves out of the midst of the stall; that chant to the sound of the viol, and invent to themselves instruments of music, like David; that drink wine in bowls, and anoint themselves with the chief ointments: but they are not grieved for the affliction of Joseph. Therefore now shall they go captive with the first that go captive, and the banquet of them that stretched themselves shall be removed.

The Lord God hath sworn by himself, saith the Lord the God of Hosts, "I abhor the excellency of Jacob, and hate his palaces: therefore will I deliver up the city with all that is therein." And it shall come to pass, if there remain ten men in one house, that they shall die. And a man's uncle shall take him up, and he that burneth him, to bring out the bones out of the house, and shall say unto him that is by the sides of the house, "Is there yet any with thee?" and he shall say, "No." Then shall he say, "Hold thy tongue: for we may not make mention of the name of the Lord."

For, behold, the Lord commandeth, and he will smite the great house with breaches, and the little house with clefts. Shall horses run upon the rock? will one plow there with oxen? for ye have turned judgment into gall, and the fruit of righteousness into hemlock, ye which rejoice in a thing of nought, which say, "Have we not taken to us horns by our own strength?" But, behold, I will raise up against you a nation, O house of Israel, saith the Lord the God of Hosts; and they shall afflict you from the entering in of Hemath unto the river of the wilderness.

Thus hath the Lord God shewed unto me; and, behold, he formed grasshoppers in the beginning of the shooting up of the latter growth; and, lo, it was the latter growth after the king's mowings. And it came to pass, that when they had made an end of eating the grass of the land, then I said, "O Lord God, forgive, I beseech thee: by whom shall Jacob arise? for he is small." The Lord repented for this: "It shall not be," saith the Lord.

Thus hath the Lord God shewed unto me: and, behold, the Lord God called to contend by fire, and it devoured the great deep, and did eat up a part. Then said I, "O Lord God, cease, I beseech thee: by whom shall Jacob arise? for he is small." The Lord repented for this: "This also shall not be," saith the Lord God.

Thus he shewed me: and, behold, the Lord stood upon a wall made by a plumbline, with a plumbline in his hand. And the Lord said unto me, "Amos, what seest thou?" And I said, "A plumbline." Then said the Lord, "Behold, I will set a plumbline in the midst of my people

Israel: I will not again pass by them any more: and the high places of Isaac shall be desolate, and the sanctuaries of Israel shall be laid waste; and I will rise against the house of Jeroboam with the sword."

Then Amaziah the priest of Beth-el sent to Jeroboam king of Israel, saying, "Amos hath conspired against thee in the midst of the house of Israel: the land is not able to bear all his words. For thus Amos saith, Jeroboam shall die by the sword, and Israel shall surely be led away captive out of their own land." Also Amaziah said unto Amos, "O thou seer, go, flee thee away into the land of Judah, and there eat bread, and prophesy there: but prophesy not again any more at Beth-el: for it is the king's chapel, and it is the king's court." Then answered Amos, and said to Amaziah, "I was no prophet, neither was I a prophet's son; but I was an herdman, and a gatherer of sycomore fruit: and the Lord took me as I followed the flock, and the Lord said unto me, Go, prophesy unto my people Israel. Now therefore hear thou the word of the Lord: Thou sayest, Prophesy not against Israel, and drop not thy word against the house of Isaac. Therefore thus saith the Lord; Thy wife shall be an harlot in the city, and thy sons and thy daughters shall fall by the sword, and thy land shall be divided by line; and thou shalt die in a polluted land: and

Israel shall surely go into captivity forth of his land."

Thus hath the Lord God shewed unto me: and behold a basket of summer fruit. And he said, "Amos, what seest thou?" And I said, "A basket of summer fruit." Then said the Lord unto me, "The end is come upon my people of Israel; I will not again pass by them any more. And the songs of the temple shall be howlings in that day, saith the Lord God: there shall be many dead bodies in every place; they shall cast them forth with silence."

Hear this, O ye that swallow up the needy, even to make the poor of the land to fail, saying, "When will the new moon be gone, that we may sell corn? and the sabbath, that we may set forth wheat, making the ephah small, and the shekel great, and falsifying the balances by deceit? that we may buy the poor for silver, and the needy for a pair of shoes; yea, and sell the refuse of the wheat?" The Lord hath sworn by the excellency of Jacob, "Surely I will never forget any of their works."

Shall not the land tremble for this, and every one mourn that dwelleth therein? and it shall rise up wholly as a flood; and it shall be cast out and drowned, as by the flood of Egypt. And it shall come to pass in that day, saith the Lord God, that I will cause the sun to go down at noon, and I will darken the earth in the clear day: and I will turn your feasts into mourning, and all your songs into lamentation; and I will bring up sackcloth upon all loins, and baldness upon every head; and I will make it as the mourning of an only son, and the end thereof as a bitter day. Behold, the days come, saith the Lord God, that I will send a famine in the land, not a famine of bread, nor a thirst for water, but of hearing the words of the Lord: and they shall wander from sea to sea, and from the north even to the east, they shall run to and fro to seek the word of the Lord, and shall not find it. In that day shall the fair virgins and young men faint for thirst. They that swear by the sin of Samaria, and say, "Thy god, O Dan, liveth;" and, "The manner of Beer-sheba liveth;" even they shall fall, and never rise up again.

I saw the Lord standing upon the altar: and he said, "Smite the lintel of the door, that the posts may shake: and cut them in the head, all of them; and I will slay the last of them with the sword: he that fleeth of them shall not flee away, and he that escapeth of them shall not be delivered. Though they dig into hell, thence shall mine hand take them; though they climb up to heaven, thence will I bring them down: and though they hide themselves in the top of Carmel, I will search and take them out thence; and though they be hid from my sight in the bottom of the sea, thence will I command the serpent, and he shall bite them: and though they go into captivity before their enemies, thence will I command the sword, and it shall slay them: and I will set mine eyes upon them for evil, and not for good."

And the Lord God of Hosts is he that toucheth the land, and it shall melt, and all that dwell therein shall mourn: and it shall rise up wholly like a flood; and shall be drowned, as by the flood of Egypt. It is he that buildeth his stories in the heaven, and hath founded his troop in the earth; he that calleth for the waters of the sea, and poureth them out upon the face of the earth: The Lord is his name.

Are ye not as children of the Ethiopians unto me, O children of Israel? saith the Lord. Have not I brought up Israel out of the land of Egypt? and the Philistines from Caphtor, and the Syrians from Kir? Behold, the eyes of the Lord God are upon the sinful kingdom, and I will destroy it from off the face of the earth; saving that I will not utterly destroy the house of Jacob, saith the Lord. For, lo, I will command, and I will sift the house of Israel among all nations, like as corn is sifted in a sieve, yet shall not the least grain fall upon the earth. All the sinners of my people shall die by the sword, which say, "The evil shall not overtake nor prevent us."

In that day will I raise up the tabernacle of

David that is fallen, and close up the breaches thereof; and I will raise up his ruins, and I will build it as in the days of old: that they may possess the remnant of Edom, and of all the heathen, which are called by my name, saith the Lord that doeth this.

Behold, the days come, saith the Lord, that the plowman shall overtake the reaper, and the treader of grapes him that soweth seed; and the mountains shall drop sweet wine, and all the hills shall melt. And I will bring again the captivity of my people of Israel, and they shall build the waste cities, and inhabit them; and they shall plant vineyards, and drink the wine thereof; they shall also make gardens, and eat the fruit of them. And I will plant them upon their land, and they shall no more be pulled up out of their land which I have given them, saith the Lord thy God.

OBADIAH

THE vision of Obadiah.

THUS saith the Lord God concerning Edom; We have heard a rumour from the Lord, and an ambassador is sent among the heathen, "Arise ye, and let us rise up against her in battle."

Behold, I have made thee small among the heathen: thou art greatly despised. The pride of thine heart hath deceived thee, thou that dwellest in the clefts of the rock, whose habitation is high; that saith in his heart, "Who shall bring me down to the ground?" Though thou exalt thyself as the eagle, and though thou set thy nest among the stars, thence will I bring thee down, saith the Lord. If thieves came to thee, if robbers by night, (how art thou cut off!) would they not have stolen till they had enough? if the grapegatherers came to thee, would they not leave some grapes? How are the things of Esau searched out! how are his hidden things sought up! All the men of thy confederacy have brought thee even to the border: the men that were at peace with thee have deceived thee, and prevailed against thee; they that eat thy bread have laid a wound under thee: there is none understanding in him.

Shall I not in that day, saith the Lord, even destroy the wise men out of Edom, and understanding out of the mount of Esau? and thy mighty men, O Teman, shall be dismayed, to the end that every one of the mount of Esau may be cut off by slaughter. For thy violence against thy brother Jacob shame shall cover thee, and thou shalt be cut off for ever.

In the day that thou stoodest on the other side, in the day that the strangers carried away captive his forces, and foreigners entered into his gates, and cast lots upon Jerusalem, even thou wast as one of them. But thou shouldest not have looked on the day of thy brother in the day that he became a stranger; neither shouldest thou have rejoiced over the children of Judah in the day of their destruction; neither shouldest thou have spoken proudly in the day of distress. Thou shouldest not have entered into the gate of my people in the day of their calamity; yea, thou shouldest not have looked on their affliction in the day of their calamity, nor have laid hands on their substance in the day of their calamity; neither shouldest thou have stood in the crossway, to cut off those of his that did escape; neither shouldest thou have delivered up those of his that did remain in the day of distress.

For the day of the Lord is near upon all the heathen: as thou hast done, it shall be done unto thee: thy reward shall return upon thine own head. For as ye have drunk upon my holy mountain, so shall all the heathen drink continually, yea, they shall drink, and they shall swallow down, and they shall be as though they had not been. But upon mount Zion shall be deliverance, and there shall be holiness; and the house of Jacob shall possess their possessions. And the house of Jacob shall be a fire, and the house of Joseph a flame, and the house of Esau for stubble, and they shall kindle in them, and devour them; and there shall not be any remaining of the house of Esau; for the Lord hath spoken it. And they of the south shall possess the mount of Esau; and they of the plain the Philistines: and they shall possess the fields of Ephraim, and the fields of Samaria: and Benjamin shall possess Gilead. And the captivity of this host of the children of Israel shall possess that of the Canaanites, even unto Zarephath; and the captivity of Jerusalem, which is in Sepharad, shall possess the cities of the south. And saviours shall come up on mount Zion to judge the mount of Esau; and the kingdom shall be the Lord's.

JONAH

NOW the word of the Lord came unto Jonah the son of Amittai, saying, "Arise, go to Nineveh, that great city, and cry against it; for their wickedness is come up before me." But Jonah rose up to flee unto Tarshish from the presence of the Lord, and went down to Joppa; and he found a ship going to Tarshish: so he paid the fare thereof, and went down into it, to go with them unto Tarshish from the presence of the Lord. But the Lord sent out a great wind into the sea, and there was a mighty tempest in the sea, so that the ship was like to be broken. Then the mariners were afraid, and cried every man unto his god, and cast forth the wares that were in the ship into the sea, to lighten it of them. But Jonah was gone down into the sides of the ship; and he lay, and was fast asleep. So the shipmaster came to him, and said unto him, "What meanest thou, O sleeper? arise, call upon thy God, if so be that God will think upon us, that we perish not." And they said every one to his fellow, "Come, and let us cast lots, that we may know for whose cause this evil is upon us." So they cast lots, and the lot fell upon Jonah. Then said they unto him, "Tell us, we pray thee, for whose cause this evil is upon us; what is thine occupation? and whence comest thou? what is thy country? and of what people art thou?" And he said unto them, "I am an Hebrew; and I fear the Lord, the God of heaven, which hath made the sea and the dry land." Then were the men exceedingly afraid, and said unto him, "Why hast thou done this?" For the men knew that he fled from the presence of the Lord, because he had told them. Then said they unto him, "What shall we do unto thee, that the sea may be calm unto us?" for the sea wrought, and was tempestuous. And he said unto them, "Take me up, and cast me forth into the sea; so shall the sea be calm unto you: for I know that for my sake this great tempest is upon you." Nevertheless the men rowed hard to bring it to the land; but they could not: for the sea wrought, and was tempestuous against them. Wherefore they cried unto the Lord, and said, "We beseech thee, O Lord, we beseech thee, let us not perish for this man's life, and lay not upon us innocent blood: for thou, O Lord, hast done as it pleased thee." So they took up Jonah, and cast him forth into the sea: and the sea ceased from her raging. Then the men feared the Lord exceedingly, and offered a sacrifice unto the Lord, and made vows.

Now the Lord had prepared a great fish to swallow up Jonah. And Jonah was in the belly of the fish three days and three nights. Then Jonah prayed unto the Lord his God out of the fish's belly, and said,

I CRIED by reason of mine affliction unto the Lord, and he heard me;
Out of the belly of hell cried I, and thou heardest my voice.
For thou hadst cast me into the deep, in the midst of the seas; and the floods compassed me about: all thy billows and thy waves passed over me.
Then I said, "I am cast out of thy sight; yet I will look again toward thy holy temple."
The waters compassed me about, even to the soul: the depth closed me round about.
The weeds were wrapped about my head: I went down to the bottoms of the mountains.
The earth with her bars was about me for ever: yet hast thou brought up my life from corruption, O Lord my God.
When my soul fainted within me I remembered the Lord: and my prayer came in unto thee, into thine holy temple.
They that observe lying vanities forsake their own mercy.
But I will sacrifice unto thee with the voice of thanksgiving; I will pay that that I have vowed.
Salvation is of the Lord.

AND the Lord spake unto the fish, and it vomited out Jonah upon the dry land. And the word of the Lord came unto Jonah the second time, saying, "Arise, go unto Nineveh, that great city, and preach unto it the preaching that I bid thee." So Jonah arose, and went unto Nineveh, according to the word of the Lord. Now Nineveh was an exceeding great city of three days' journey. And Jonah began to enter into the city a day's journey, and he cried, and said, "Yet forty days, and Nineveh shall be overthrown."

So the people of Nineveh believed God, and proclaimed a fast, and put on sackcloth, from the greatest of them even to the least of them. For word came unto the king of Nineveh, and he arose from his throne, and he laid his robe from him, and covered him with sackcloth, and sat in ashes. And he caused it to be proclaimed and published through Nineveh by the decree of the king and his nobles, saying, "Let neither man nor beast, herd nor flock, taste any thing: let them not feed, nor drink water: but let man and beast be covered with sackcloth, and cry mightily unto God: yea, let them turn every one from his evil way, and from the violence that is in their hands. Who can tell if God will turn and repent, and turn away from his fierce anger, that we perish not?"

And God saw their works, that they turned

from their evil way; and God repented of the evil, that he had said that he would do unto them; and he did it not. But it displeased Jonah exceedingly, and he was very angry. And he prayed unto the Lord, and said, "I pray thee, O Lord, was not this my saying, when I was yet in my country? therefore I fled before unto Tarshish: for I knew that thou art a gracious God, and merciful, slow to anger, and of great kindness, and repentest thee of the evil. Therefore now, O Lord, take, I beseech thee, my life from me; for it is better for me to die than to live."

Then said the Lord, "Doest thou well to be angry?" So Jonah went out of the city, and sat on the east side of the city, and there made him a booth, and sat under it in the shadow, till he might see what would become of the city. And the Lord God prepared a gourd, and made it to come up over Jonah, that it might be a shadow over his head, to deliver him from his grief. So Jonah was exceeding glad of the gourd. But God prepared a worm when the morning rose the next day, and it smote the gourd that it withered. And it came to pass, when the sun did arise, that God prepared a vehement east wind; and the sun beat upon the head of Jonah, that he fainted, and wished in himself to die, and said, "It is better for me to die than to live." And God said to Jonah, "Doest thou well to be angry for the gourd?" And he said, "I do well to be angry, even unto death." Then said the Lord, "Thou hast had pity on the gourd, for the which thou hast not laboured, neither madest it grow; which came up in a night, and perished in a night: and should not I spare Nineveh, that great city, wherein are more than sixscore thousand persons that cannot discern between their right hand and their left hand; and also much cattle?"

MICAH

THE word of the Lord that came to Micah the Morasthite in the days of Jotham, Ahaz, and Hezekiah, kings of Judah, which he saw concerning Samaria and Jerusalem.

HEAR, all ye people; hearken, O earth, and all that therein is: and let the Lord God be witness against you, the Lord from his holy temple. For, behold, the Lord cometh forth out of his place, and will come down, and tread upon the high places of the earth. And the mountains shall be molten under him, and the valleys shall be cleft, as wax before the fire, and as the waters that are poured down a steep place.

For the transgression of Jacob is all this, and for the sins of the house of Israel. What is the transgression of Jacob? is it not Samaria? and what are the high places of Judah? are they not Jerusalem? Therefore I will make Samaria as an heap of the field, and as plantings of a vineyard: and I will pour down the stones thereof into the valley, and I will discover the foundations thereof. And all the graven images thereof shall be beaten to pieces, and all the hires thereof shall be burned with the fire, and all the idols thereof will I lay desolate: for she gathered it of the hire of an harlot, and they shall return to the hire of an harlot. Therefore I will wail and howl, I will go stripped and naked: I will make a wailing like the dragons, and mourning as the owls. For her wound is incurable; for it is come unto Judah; he is come unto the gate of my people, even to Jerusalem.

Declare ye it not at Gath, weep ye not at all: in the house of Aphrah roll thyself in the dust. Pass ye away, thou inhabitant of Saphir, having thy shame naked: the inhabitant of Zaanan came not forth in the mourning of Beth-ezel; he shall receive of you his standing. For the inhabitant of Maroth waited carefully for good: but evil came down from the Lord unto the gate of Jerusalem. O thou inhabitant of Lachish, bind the chariot to the swift beast: she is the beginning of the sin to the daughter of Zion: for the transgressions of Israel were found in thee. Therefore shalt thou give presents to Moresheth-gath: the houses of Achzib shall be a lie to the kings of Israel. Yet will I bring an heir unto thee, O inhabitant of Mareshah: he shall come unto Adullam the glory of Israel. Make thee bald, and poll thee for thy delicate children: enlarge thy baldness as the eagle; for they are gone into captivity from thee.

Woe to them that devise iniquity, and work

evil upon their beds! when the morning is light, they practise it, because it is in the power of their hand: and they covet fields, and take them by violence; and houses, and take them away: so they oppress a man and his house, even a man and his heritage. Therefore thus saith the Lord; Behold, against this family do I devise an evil, from which ye shall not remove your necks; neither shall ye go haughtily: for this time is evil. In that day shall one take up a parable against you, and lament with a doleful lamentation, and say, "We be utterly spoiled: he hath changed the portion of my people: how hath he removed it from me! turning away he hath divided our fields." Therefore thou shalt have none that shall cast a cord by lot in the congregation of the Lord.

"Prophesy ye not," say they to them that prophesy: they shall not prophesy to them, that they shall not take shame. O thou that art named the house of Jacob, is the spirit of the Lord straitened? are these his doings? do not my words do good to him that walketh uprightly? Even of late my people is risen up as an enemy: ye pull off the robe with the garment from them that pass by securely as men averse from war. The women of my people have ye cast out from their pleasant houses; from their children have ye taken away my glory for ever. Arise ye and depart; for this is not your rest: because it is polluted, it shall destroy you, even with a sore destruction. If a man walking in the spirit and falsehood do lie, saying, "I will prophesy unto thee of wine and of strong drink;" he shall even be the prophet of this people.

I will surely assemble, O Jacob, all of thee; I will surely gather the remnant of Israel; I will put them together as the sheep of Bozrah, as the flock in the midst of their fold: they shall make great noise by reason of the multitude of men. The breaker is come up before them: they have broken up, and have passed through the gate, and are gone out by it: and their king shall pass before them, and the Lord on the head of them.

And I said, "Hear, I pray you, O heads of Jacob, and ye princes of the house of Israel; is it not for you to know judgment? who hate the good, and love the evil; who pluck off their skin from off them, and their flesh from off their bones; who also eat the flesh of my people, and flay their skin from off them; and they break their bones, and chop them in pieces, as for the pot, and as flesh within the caldron." Then shall they cry unto the Lord, but he will not hear them: he will even hide his face from them at that time, as they have behaved themselves ill in their doings.

Thus saith the Lord concerning the prophets

that make my people err, that bite with their teeth, and cry, "Peace;" and he that putteth not into their mouths, they even prepare war against him: therefore night shall be unto you, that ye shall not have a vision; and it shall be dark unto you, that ye shall not divine; and the sun shall go down over the prophets, and the day shall be dark over them. Then shall the seers be ashamed, and the diviners confounded: yea, they shall all cover their lips; for there is no answer of God.

But truly I am full of power by the spirit of the Lord, and of judgment, and of might, to declare unto Jacob his transgression, and to Israel his sin. Hear this, I pray you, ye heads of the house of Jacob, and princes of the house of Israel, that abhor judgment, and pervert all equity. They build up Zion with blood, and Jerusalem with iniquity: the heads thereof judge for reward, and the priests thereof teach for hire, and the prophets thereof divine for money: yet will they lean upon the Lord, and say, "Is not the Lord among us? none evil can come upon us." Therefore shall Zion for your sake be plowed as a field, and Jerusalem shall become heaps, and the mountain of the house as the high places of the forest.

But in the last days it shall come to pass, that the mountain of the house of the Lord shall be established in the top of the mountains, and it shall be exalted above the hills; and people shall flow unto it. And many nations shall come, and say, "Come, and let us go up to the mountain of the Lord, and to the house of the God of Jacob; and he will teach us of his ways, and we will walk in his paths:" for the law shall go forth of Zion, and the word of the Lord from Jerusalem. And he shall judge among many people, and rebuke strong nations afar off; and they shall beat their swords into plowshares, and their spears into pruninghooks: nation shall not lift up a sword against nation, neither shall they learn war any more. But they shall sit every man under his vine and under his fig tree; and none shall make them afraid: for the mouth of the Lord of Hosts hath spoken it. For all people will walk every one in the name of his god, and we will walk in the name of the Lord our God for ever and ever.

In that day, saith the Lord, will I assemble her that halteth, and I will gather her that is driven out, and her that I have afflicted; and I will make her that halted a remnant, and her that was cast far off a strong nation: and the Lord shall reign over them in mount Zion from henceforth, even for ever. And thou, O tower of the flock, the strong hold of the daughter of Zion, unto thee shall it come, even the first dominion; the kingdom shall come to the daughter of Jerusalem.

Now why dost thou cry out aloud? is there no king in thee? is thy counsellor perished? for pangs have taken thee as a woman in travail. Be in pain, and labour to bring forth, O daughter of Zion, like a woman in travail: for now shalt thou go forth out of the city, and thou shalt dwell in the field, and thou shalt go even to Babylon; there shalt thou be delivered; there the Lord shall redeem thee from the hand of thine enemies. Now also many nations are gathered against thee, that say, "Let her be defiled, and let our eye look upon Zion." But they know not the thoughts of the Lord, neither understand they his counsel: for he shall gather them as the sheaves into the floor. Arise and thresh, O daughter of Zion: for I will make thine horn iron, and I will make thy hoofs brass: and thou shalt beat in pieces many people: and I will consecrate their gain unto the Lord, and their substance unto the Lord of the whole earth.

Now gather thyself in troops, O daughter of troops: he hath laid siege against us: they shall smite the judge of Israel with a rod upon the cheek. But thou, Beth-lehem Ephratah, though thou be little among the thousands of Judah, yet out of thee shall he come forth unto me that is to be ruler in Israel; whose goings forth have been from of old, from everlasting. Therefore will he give them up, until the time that she which travaileth hath brought forth: then the remnant of his brethren shall return unto the children of Israel. And he shall stand and feed in the strength of the Lord, in the majesty of the name of the Lord his God; and they shall abide: for now shall he be great unto the ends of the earth. And this man shall be the peace, when the Assyrian shall come into our land: and when he shall tread in our palaces, then shall we raise against him seven shepherds, and eight principal men. And they shall waste the land of Assyria with the sword, and the land of Nimrod in the entrances thereof: thus shall he deliver us from the Assyrian, when he cometh into our land, and when he treadeth within our borders.

And the remnant of Jacob shall be in the midst of many people as a dew from the Lord, as the showers upon the grass, that tarrieth not for man, nor waiteth for the sons of men. And the remnant of Jacob shall be among the Gentiles in the midst of many people as a lion among the beasts of the forest, as a young lion among the flocks of sheep: who, if he go through, both treadeth down, and teareth in pieces, and none can deliver. Thine hand shall be lifted up upon thine adversaries, and all thine enemies shall be cut off. And it shall come to pass in that day, saith the Lord, that I will cut off thy horses out of the midst of thee, and I will destroy thy chariots. And I will cut off the cities of thy land, and throw down all thy strong holds: and I will cut off witchcrafts out of thine hand, and thou shalt have no more soothsayers; thy graven images also will I cut off, and thy standing images out of the midst of thee; and thou shalt no more worship the work of thine hands. And I will pluck up thy groves out of the midst of thee: so will I destroy thy cities. And I will execute vengeance in anger and fury upon the heathen, such as they have not heard.

Hear ye now what the Lord saith; Arise, contend thou before the mountains, and let the hills hear thy voice. Hear ye, O mountains, the Lord's controversy, and ye strong foundations of the earth: for the Lord hath a controversy with his people, and he will plead with Israel.

O my people, what have I done unto thee? and wherein have I wearied thee? testify against me. For I brought thee up out of the land of Egypt, and redeemed thee out of the house of servants; and I sent before thee Moses, Aaron, and Miriam.

O my people, remember now what Balak king of Moab consulted, and what Balaam the son of Beor answered him from Shittim unto Gilgal; that ye may know the righteousness of the Lord. "Wherewith shall I come before the Lord, and bow myself before the high God?

shall I come before him with burnt offerings, with calves of a year old? will the Lord be pleased with thousands of rams, or with ten thousands of rivers of oil? shall I give my firstborn for my transgression, the fruit of my body for the sin of my soul?" "He hath shewed thee, O man, what is good; and what doth the Lord require of thee, but to do justly, and to love mercy, and to walk humbly with thy God?"

The Lord's voice crieth unto the city, and the man of wisdom shall see thy name: hear ye the rod, and who hath appointed it. Are there yet the treasures of wickedness in the house of the wicked, and the scant measure that is abominable? shall I count them pure with the wicked balances, and with the bag of deceitful weights? for the rich men thereof are full of violence, and the inhabitants thereof have spoken lies, and their tongue is deceitful in their mouth. Therefore also will I make thee sick in smiting thee, in making thee desolate because of thy sins. Thou shalt eat, but not be satisfied; and thy casting down shall be in the midst of thee; and thou shalt take hold, but shalt not deliver; and that which thou deliverest will I give up to the sword. Thou shalt sow, but thou shalt not reap; thou shalt tread the olives, but thou shalt not anoint thee with oil; and sweet wine, but shalt not drink wine. For the statutes of Omri are kept, and all the works of the house of Ahab, and ye walk in their counsels; that I should make thee a desolation, and the inhabitants thereof an hissing: therefore ye shall bear the reproach of my people.

Woe is me! for I am as when they have gathered the summer fruits, as the grapegleanings of the vintage: there is no cluster to eat: my soul desired the firstripe fruit. The good man is perished out of the earth: and there is none upright among men: they all lie in wait for blood; they hunt every man his brother with a net. That they may do evil with both hands earnestly, the prince asketh, and the judge asketh for a reward; and the great man, he uttereth his mischievous desire: so they wrap it up. The best of them is as a brier: the most upright is sharper than a thorn hedge: the day of thy watchmen and thy visitation cometh; now shall be their perplexity. Trust ye not in a friend, put ye not confidence in a guide: keep the doors of thy mouth from her that lieth in thy bosom. For the son dishonoureth the father, the daughter riseth up against her mother, the daughter in law against her mother in law; a man's enemies are the men of his own house.

Therefore I will look unto the Lord; I will wait for the God of my salvation: my God will hear me. Rejoice not against me, O mine enemy: when I fall, I shall arise; when I sit in darkness, the Lord shall be a light unto me. I will bear the indignation of the Lord, because I have sinned against him, until he plead my cause, and execute judgment for me: he will bring me forth to the light, and I shall behold his righteousness. Then she that is mine enemy shall see it, and shame shall cover her which said unto me, "Where is the Lord thy God?" mine eyes shall behold her: now shall she be trodden down as the mire of the streets.

In the day that thy walls are to be built, in that day shall the decree be far removed. In that day also he shall come even to thee from Assyria, and from the fortified cities, and from the fortress even to the river, and from sea to sea, and from mountain to mountain. Notwithstanding the land shall be desolate because of them that dwell therein, for the fruit of their doings.

Feed thy people with thy rod, the flock of thine heritage, which dwell solitarily in the wood, in the midst of Carmel: let them feed in Bashan and Gilead, as in the days of old.

According to the days of thy coming out of the land of Egypt will I shew unto him marvellous things.

The nations shall see and be confounded at all their might: they shall lay their hand upon their mouth, their ears shall be deaf. They shall lick the dust like a serpent, they shall move out of their holes like worms of the earth: they shall be afraid of the Lord our God, and shall fear because of thee. Who is a God like unto thee, that pardoneth iniquity, and passeth by the transgression of the remnant of his heritage? he retaineth not his anger for ever, because he delighteth in mercy. He will turn again, he will have compassion upon us; he will subdue our iniquities; and thou wilt cast all their sins into the depths of the sea. Thou wilt perform the truth to Jacob, and the mercy to Abraham, which thou hast sworn unto our fathers from the days of old.

NAHUM

THE burden of Nineveh. The book of the vision of Nahum the Elkoshite.

GOD is jealous, and the Lord revengeth; the Lord revengeth, and is furious; the Lord will take vengeance on his adversaries, and he reserveth wrath for his enemies. The Lord is slow to anger, and great in power, and will not at all acquit the wicked: the Lord hath his way in the whirlwind and in the storm, and the clouds are the dust of his feet. He rebuketh the sea, and maketh it dry, and drieth up all the rivers: Bashan languisheth, and Carmel, and the flower of Lebanon languisheth. The mountains quake at him, and the hills melt, and the earth is burned at his presence, yea, the world, and all that dwell therein. Who can stand before his indignation? and who can abide in the fierceness of his anger? his fury is poured out like fire, and the rocks are thrown down by him.

The Lord is good, a strong hold in the day of trouble; and he knoweth them that trust in him. But with an overrunning flood he will make an utter end of the place thereof, and darkness shall pursue his enemies. What do ye imagine against the Lord? he will make an utter end: affliction shall not rise up the second time. For while they be folden together as thorns, and while they are drunken as drunkards, they shall be devoured as stubble fully dry. There is one come out of thee, that imagineth evil against the Lord, a wicked counsellor. Thus saith the Lord; Though they be quiet, and likewise many, yet thus shall they be cut down, when he shall pass through.

Though I have afflicted thee, I will afflict thee no more; for now will I break his yoke from off thee, and will burst thy bonds in sunder.

And the Lord hath given a commandment concerning thee, that no more of thy name be sown: out of the house of thy gods will I cut off the graven image and the molten image: I will make thy grave; for thou art vile.

Behold upon the mountains the feet of him that bringeth good tidings, that publisheth peace! O Judah, keep thy solemn feasts, perform thy vows: for the wicked shall no more pass through thee; he is utterly cut off.

He that dasheth in pieces is come up before thy face: keep the munition, watch the way, make thy loins strong, fortify thy power mightily. For the Lord hath turned away the excellency of Jacob, as the excellency of Israel: for the emptiers have emptied them out, and marred their vine branches.

The shield of his mighty men is made red, the valiant men are in scarlet: the chariots shall be with flaming torches in the day of his preparation, and the fir trees shall be terribly shaken. The chariots shall rage in the streets, they shall justle one against another in the broad ways: they shall seem like torches, they shall run like the lightnings. He shall recount his worthies: they shall stumble in their walk; they shall make haste to the wall thereof, and the defence shall be prepared.

The gates of the rivers shall be opened, and the palace shall be dissolved. And Huzzab shall be led away captive, she shall be brought up, and her maids shall lead her as with the voice of doves, tabering upon their breasts.

But Nineveh is of old like a pool of water: yet they shall flee away. "Stand, stand!" shall they cry; but none shall look back. Take ye the spoil of silver, take the spoil of gold: for there is none end of the store and glory out of all the pleasant furniture. She is empty, and void, and waste: and the heart melteth, and the knees smite together, and much pain is in all loins, and the faces of them all gather blackness.

Where is the dwelling of the lions, and the feedingplace of the young lions, where the lion, even the old lion, walked, and the lion's whelp, and none made them afraid? the lion did tear in pieces enough for his whelps, and strangled for his lionesses, and filled his holes with prey, and his dens with ravin. Behold, I am against thee, saith the Lord of Hosts, and I will burn her chariots in the smoke, and the sword shall devour thy young lions: and I will cut off thy prey from the earth, and the voice of thy messengers shall no more be heard. Woe to the bloody city! it is all full of lies and robbery; the prey departeth not.

The noise of a whip, and the noise of the rattling of the wheels, and of the prancing horses, and of the jumping chariots! The horseman lifteth up both the bright sword and the glittering spear: and there is a multitude of slain, and a great number of carcases; and there is none end of their corpses; they stumble upon their corpses: because of the multitude of the whoredoms of the wellfavoured harlot, the mistress of witchcrafts, that selleth nations through her whoredoms, and families through her witchcrafts.

Behold, I am against thee, saith the Lord of Hosts; and I will discover thy skirts upon thy face, and I will shew the nations thy nakedness, and the kingdoms thy shame. And I will cast abominable filth upon thee, and make thee vile, and will set thee as a gazingstock. And it shall come to pass, that all they that look upon thee shall flee from thee, and say, "Nineveh is laid waste: who will bemoan her?"

Whence shall I seek comforters for thee? art
thou better than populous No, that was situate
among the rivers, that had the waters round
about it, whose rampart was the sea, and her
wall was from the sea? Ethiopia and Egypt
were her strength, and it was infinite; Put and
Lubim were thy helpers. Yet was she carried
away, she went into captivity: her young children also were dashed in pieces at the top of all
the streets: and they cast lots for her honourable
men, and all her great men were bound in
chains.

Thou also shalt be drunken: thou shalt be
hid, thou also shalt seek strength because of
the enemy. All thy strong holds shall be like
fig trees with the firstripe figs: if they be
shaken, they shall even fall into the mouth of
the eater. Behold, thy people in the midst of
thee are women: the gates of thy land shall be
set wide open unto thine enemies: the fire shall
devour thy bars. Draw thee waters for the
siege, fortify thy strong holds: go into clay,
and tread the mortar, make strong the brickkiln. There shall the fire devour thee; the
sword shall cut thee off, it shall eat thee up
like the cankerworm. Make thyself many as the
cankerworm, make thyself many as the locusts:
thou hast multiplied thy merchants above the
stars of heaven: the cankerworm spoileth, and
fleeth away. Thy crowned are as the locusts,

and thy captains as the great grasshoppers, which camp in the hedges in the cold day, but when the sun ariseth they flee away, and their place is not known where they are.

Thy shepherds slumber, O king of Assyria: thy nobles shall dwell in the dust: thy people is scattered upon the mountains, and no man gathereth them. There is no healing of thy bruise; thy wound is grievous: all that hear the bruit of thee shall clap the hands over thee: for upon whom hath not thy wickedness passed continually?

HABAKKUK

THE burden which Habakkuk the prophet did see.

O LORD, how long shall I cry, and thou wilt not hear! even cry out unto thee of violence, and thou wilt not save! Why dost thou shew me iniquity, and cause me to behold grievance? for spoiling and violence are before me: and there are that raise up strife and contention. Therefore the law is slacked, and judgment doth never go forth: for the wicked doth compass about the righteous; therefore wrong judgment proceedeth.

Behold ye among the heathen, and regard, and wonder marvellously: for I will work a work in your days, which ye will not believe, though it be told you. For, lo, I raise up the Chaldeans, that bitter and hasty nation, which shall march through the breadth of the land, to possess the dwellingplaces that are not theirs. They are terrible and dreadful: their judgment and their dignity shall proceed of themselves. Their horses also are swifter than the leopards, and are more fierce than the evening wolves: and their horsemen shall spread themselves, and their horsemen shall come from far; they shall fly as the eagle that hasteth to eat. They shall come all for violence: their faces shall sup up as the east wind, and they shall gather the captivity as the sand. And they shall scoff at the kings, and the princes shall be a scorn unto them: they shall deride every strong hold; for they shall heap dust, and take it. Then shall his mind change, and he shall pass over, and offend, imputing this his power unto his god.

Art thou not from everlasting, O Lord my God, mine Holy One? we shall not die. O Lord, thou hast ordained them for judgment; and, O mighty God, thou hast established them for correction. Thou art of purer eyes than to behold evil, and canst not look on iniquity: wherefore lookest thou upon them that deal treacherously, and holdest thy tongue when the wicked devoureth the man that is more righteous than he? and makest men as the fishes of the sea, as the creeping things, that have no ruler over them?

They take up all of them with the angle, they catch them in their net, and gather them in their drag: therefore they rejoice and are glad. Therefore they sacrifice unto their net, and burn incense unto their drag; because by them their portion is fat, and their meat plenteous. Shall they therefore empty their net, and not spare continually to slay the nations?

I will stand upon my watch, and set me

upon the tower, and will watch to see what he will say unto me, and what I shall answer when I am reproved.

And the Lord answered me, and said, "Write the vision, and make it plain upon tables, that he may run that readeth it. For the vision is yet for an appointed time, but at the end it shall speak, and not lie: though it tarry, wait for it; because it will surely come, it will not tarry."

Behold, his soul which is lifted up is not upright in him: but the just shall live by his faith. Yea also, because he transgresseth by wine, he is a proud man, neither keepeth at home, who enlargeth his desire as hell, and is as death, and cannot be satisfied, but gathereth unto him all nations, and heapeth unto him all people: shall not all these take up a parable against him, and a taunting proverb against him, and say, "Woe to him that increaseth that which is not his! how long? and to him that ladeth himself with thick clay!" Shall they not rise up suddenly that shall bite thee, and awake that shall vex thee, and thou shalt be for booties unto them? because thou hast spoiled many nations, all the remnant of the people shall spoil thee; because of men's blood, and for the violence of the land, of the city, and of all that dwell therein.

Woe to him that coveteth an evil covetousness to his house, that he may set his nest on high, that he may be delivered from the power of evil! Thou hast consulted shame to thy house by cutting off many people, and hast sinned against thy soul. For the stone shall cry out of the wall, and the beam out of the timber shall answer it.

Woe to him that buildeth a town with blood, and stablisheth a city by iniquity! Behold, is it not of the Lord of Hosts that the people shall labour in the very fire, and the people shall weary themselves for very vanity? for the earth shall be filled with the knowledge of the glory of the Lord, as the waters cover the sea.

Woe unto him that giveth his neighbour drink, that puttest thy bottle to him, and makest him drunken also, that thou mayest look on their nakedness! Thou art filled with shame for glory: drink thou also, and let thy foreskin be uncovered: the cup of the Lord's right hand shall be turned unto thee, and shameful spewing shall be on thy glory. For the violence of Lebanon shall cover thee, and the spoil of beasts, which made them afraid, because of men's blood, and for the violence of the land, of the city, and of all that dwell therein.

What profiteth the graven image that the maker thereof hath graven it; the molten image, and a teacher of lies, that the maker of his work trusteth therein, to make dumb idols? Woe unto him that saith to the wood, "Awake!" to the dumb stone, "Arise, it shall teach!" Behold, it is laid over with gold and silver, and there is no breath at all in the midst of it. But the Lord is in his holy temple: let all the earth keep silence before him.

A PRAYER of Habakkuk the prophet upon Shigionoth.

O LORD, I have heard thy speech, and was afraid.
O Lord, revive thy work in the midst of the years, in the midst of the years make known; in wrath remember mercy.
God came from Teman, and the Holy One from mount Paran.
His glory covered the heavens, and the earth was full of his praise, and his brightness was as the light.
He had horns coming out of his hand: and there was the hiding of his power.
Before him went the pestilence, and burning coals went forth at his feet.
He stood, and measured the earth: he beheld, and drove asunder the nations;
And the everlasting mountains were scattered, the perpetual hills did bow: his ways are everlasting.

I saw the tents of Cushan in affliction: and the curtains of the land of Midian did tremble.

Was the Lord displeased against the rivers? was thine anger against the rivers? Was thy wrath against the sea, that thou didst ride upon thine horses and thy chariots of salvation?

Thy bow was made quite naked, according to the oaths of the tribes, even thy word.

Thou didst cleave the earth with rivers: the mountains saw thee, and they trembled.

The overflowing of the water passed by: the deep uttered his voice, and lifted up his hands on high.

The sun and moon stood still in their habitation: at the light of thine arrows they went, and at the shining of thy glittering spear.

Thou didst march through the land in indignation, thou didst thresh the heathen in anger.

Thou wentest forth for the salvation of thy people, even for salvation with thine anointed;

Thou woundedst the head out of the house of the wicked, by discovering the foundation unto the neck: thou didst strike through with his staves the head of his villages.

They came out as a whirlwind to scatter me: their rejoicing was as to devour the poor secretly.

Thou didst walk through the sea with thine horses, through the heap of great waters.

When I heard, my belly trembled; my lips quivered at the voice:

Rottenness entered into my bones, and I trembled in myself, that I might rest in the day of trouble.

When he cometh up unto the people, he will invade them with his troops.

Although the fig tree shall not blossom, neither shall fruit be in the vines;

The labour of the olive shall fail, and the fields shall yield no meat;

The flock shall be cut off from the fold, and there shall be no herd in the stalls:

Yet I will rejoice in the Lord, I will joy in the God of my salvation.

The Lord God is my strength, and he will make my feet like hinds' feet, and he will make me to walk upon mine high places.

To the chief singer on my stringed instruments.

ZEPHANIAH

THE word of the Lord which came unto Zephaniah the son of Cushi, the son of Gedaliah, the son of Amariah, the son of Hizkiah, in the days of Josiah the son of Amon king of Judah.

I WILL utterly consume all things from off the land, saith the Lord. I will consume man and beast; I will consume the fowls of the heaven, and the fishes of the sea, and the stumblingblocks with the wicked; and I will cut off man from off the land, saith the Lord. I will also stretch out mine hand upon Judah, and upon all the inhabitants of Jerusalem; and I will cut off the remnant of Baal from this place, and the name of the Chemarims with the priests; and them that worship the host of heaven upon the housetops; and them that worship and that swear by the Lord, and that swear by Malcham; and them that are turned back from the Lord; and those that have not sought the Lord, nor enquired for him.

Hold thy peace at the presence of the Lord God: for the day of the Lord is at hand: for the Lord hath prepared a sacrifice, he hath bid his guests. And it shall come to pass in the day of the Lord's sacrifice, that I will punish the princes, and the king's children, and all such as are clothed with strange apparel. In the same day also will I punish all those that leap on the threshold, which fill their masters' houses with violence and deceit. And it shall come to pass in that day, saith the Lord, that there shall be the noise of a cry from the fish gate, and an howling from the second, and a great crashing from the hills. Howl, ye inhabitants of Maktesh, for all the merchant people are cut down; all they that bear silver are cut off. And it shall come to pass at that time, that I will search Jerusalem with candles, and punish the men that are settled on their lees: that say in their heart, "The Lord will not do good, neither will he do evil." Therefore their goods shall become a booty, and their houses a desolation: they shall also build houses, but not inhabit them; and they shall plant vineyards, but not drink the wine thereof.

The great day of the Lord is near, it is near, and hasteth greatly, even the voice of the day of the Lord: the mighty man shall cry there bitterly. That day is a day of wrath, a day of trouble and distress, a day of wasteness and desolation, a day of darkness and gloominess, a day of clouds and thick darkness, a day of the trumpet and alarm against the fenced cities, and against the high towers. And I will bring distress upon men, that they shall walk like blind men, because they have sinned against the Lord: and their blood shall be poured out as dust, and their flesh as the dung. Neither their silver nor their gold shall be able to deliver them in the day of the Lord's wrath; but the whole land shall be devoured by the fire of his jealousy: for he shall make even a speedy riddance of all them that dwell in the land.

Gather yourselves together, yea, gather together, O nation not desired; before the decree bring forth, before the day pass as the chaff, before the fierce anger of the Lord come upon you, before the day of the Lord's anger come upon you. Seek ye the Lord, all ye meek of the earth, which have wrought his judgment; seek righteousness, seek meekness: it may be ye shall be hid in the day of the Lord's anger.

For Gaza shall be forsaken, and Ashkelon a desolation: they shall drive out Ashdod at the noon day, and Ekron shall be rooted up. Woe unto the inhabitants of the sea coast, the nation of the Cherethites! the word of the Lord is against you; O Canaan, the land of the Philistines, I will even destroy thee, that there shall be no inhabitant. And the sea coast shall be dwellings and cottages for shepherds, and folds for flocks. And the coast shall be for the remnant of the house of Judah; they shall feed thereupon: in the houses of Ashkelon shall they lie down in the evening: for the Lord their God shall visit them, and turn away their captivity.

I have heard the reproach of Moab, and the revilings of the children of Ammon, whereby they have reproached my people, and magnified themselves against their border. Therefore as I live, saith the Lord of Hosts, the God of Israel, surely Moab shall be as Sodom, and the children of Ammon as Gomorrah, even the breeding of nettles, and saltpits, and a perpetual desolation: the residue of my people shall spoil them, and the remnant of my people shall possess them. This shall they have for their pride, because they have reproached and magnified themselves against the people of the Lord of Hosts. The Lord will be terrible unto them: for he will famish all the gods of the earth; and men shall worship him, every one from his place, even all the isles of the heathen.

Ye Ethiopians also, ye shall be slain by my sword.

And he will stretch out his hand against the north, and destroy Assyria; and will make Nineveh a desolation, and dry like a wilderness. And flocks shall lie down in the midst of her, all the beasts of the nations: both the cormorant and the bittern shall lodge in the upper lintels of it; their voice shall sing in the windows; desolation shall be in the thresholds: for he shall uncover the cedar work. This is the rejoicing city that dwelt carelessly, that said in her heart, " I am, and there is none beside me:" how is she become a desolation, a place for beasts to lie down in! every one that passeth by her shall hiss, and wag his hand.

Woe to her that is filthy and polluted, to the oppressing city! she obeyed not the voice; she received not correction; she trusted not in the Lord; she drew not near to her God. Her princes within her are roaring lions; her judges are evening wolves; they gnaw not the bones till the morrow. Her prophets are light and treacherous persons: her priests have polluted the sanctuary, they have done violence to the law. The just Lord is in the midst thereof; he will not do iniquity: every morning doth he bring his judgment to light, he faileth not; but the unjust knoweth no shame.

I have cut off the nations: their towers are desolate; I made their streets waste, that none passeth by: their cities are destroyed, so that there is no man, that there is none inhabitant. I said, " Surely thou wilt fear me, thou wilt receive instruction;" so their dwelling should not be cut off, howsoever I punished them: but they rose early, and corrupted all their doings. Therefore wait ye upon me, saith the Lord, until the day that I rise up to the prey: for my determination is to gather the nations, that I may assemble the kingdoms, to pour upon them mine indignation, even all my fierce anger: for all the earth shall be devoured with the fire of my jealousy.

For then will I turn to the people a pure language, that they may all call upon the name of the Lord, to serve him with one consent. From beyond the rivers of Ethiopia my suppliants, even the daughter of my dispersed, shall bring mine offering.

In that day shalt thou not be ashamed for all thy doings, wherein thou hast transgressed against me: for then I will take away out of the midst of thee them that rejoice in thy pride, and thou shalt no more be haughty because of my holy mountain. I will also leave in the midst of thee an afflicted and poor people, and they shall trust in the name of the Lord. The remnant of Israel shall not do iniquity, nor speak lies; neither shall a deceitful tongue be found in their mouth: for they shall feed and lie down, and none shall make them afraid.

Sing, O daughter of Zion; shout, O Israel; be glad and rejoice with all the heart, O daughter of Jerusalem. The Lord hath taken away thy judgments, he hath cast out thine enemy: the king of Israel, even the Lord, is in the midst of thee: thou shalt not see evil any more. In that day it shall be said to Jerusalem, "Fear thou not:" and to Zion, "Let not thine hands be slack." The Lord thy God in the midst of thee is mighty; he will save, he will rejoice over thee with joy; he will rest in his love, he will joy over thee with singing.

I will gather them that are sorrowful for the solemn assembly, who are of thee, to whom the reproach of it was a burden. Behold, at that time I will undo all that afflict thee: and I will save her that halteth, and gather her that was driven out; and I will get them praise and fame in every land where they have been put to shame. At that time will I bring you again, even in the time that I gather you : for I will make you a name and a praise among all people of the earth, when I turn back your captivity before your eyes, saith the Lord.

HAGGAI

IN the second year of Darius the king, in the sixth month, in the first day of the month, came the word of the Lord by Haggai the prophet unto Zerubbabel the son of Shealtiel, governor of Judah, and to Joshua the son of Josedech, the high priest, saying, "Thus speaketh the Lord of Hosts, saying, This people say, The time is not come, the time that the Lord's house should be built."

Then came the word of the Lord by Haggai the prophet, saying, "Is it time for you, O ye, to dwell in your cieled houses, and this house lie waste? Now therefore thus saith the Lord of Hosts; Consider your ways. Ye have sown much, and bring in little; ye eat, but ye have not enough; ye drink, but ye are not filled with drink; ye clothe you, but there is none warm; and he that earneth wages earneth wages to put it into a bag with holes. Thus saith the Lord of Hosts; Consider your ways.

"Go up to the mountain, and bring wood, and build the house; and I will take pleasure in it, and I will be glorified, saith the Lord. Ye looked for much, and, lo, it came to little; and when ye brought it home, I did blow upon it. Why? saith the Lord of Hosts. Because of mine house that is waste, and ye run every man unto his own house. Therefore the heaven over you is stayed from dew, and the earth is stayed from her fruit. And I called for a drought upon the land, and upon the mountains, and upon the corn, and upon the new wine, and upon the oil, and upon that which the ground bringeth forth, and upon men, and upon cattle, and upon all the labour of the hands."

Then Zerubbabel the son of Shealtiel, and Joshua the son of Josedech, the high priest, with all the remnant of the people, obeyed the voice of the Lord their God, and the words of Haggai the prophet, as the Lord their God had sent him, and the people did fear before the Lord.

Then spake Haggai the Lord's messenger in the Lord's message unto the people, saying, " I am with you, saith the Lord." And the Lord stirred up the spirit of Zerubbabel the son of Shealtiel, governor of Judah, and the spirit of Joshua the son of Josedech, the high priest, and the spirit of all the remnant of the people; and they came and did work in the house of the Lord of Hosts, their God, in the four and twentieth day of the sixth month, in the second year of Darius the king.

In the seventh month, in the one and twentieth day of the month, came the word of the Lord by the prophet Haggai, saying,

"Speak now to Zerubbabel the son of Shealtiel, governor of Judah, and to Joshua the son of Josedech, the high priest, and to the residue of the people, saying, Who is left among you that saw this house in her first glory? and how do ye see it now? is it not in your eyes in comparison of it as nothing? Yet now be strong, O Zerubbabel, saith the Lord; and be strong, O Joshua, son of Josedech, the high priest; and be strong, all ye people of the land, saith the Lord, and work: for I am with you, saith the Lord of Hosts: according to the word that I covenanted with you when ye came out of Egypt, so my spirit remaineth among you: fear ye not. For thus saith the Lord of Hosts; Yet once, it is a little while, and I will shake the heavens, and the earth, and the sea, and the dry land; and I will shake all nations, and the desire of all nations shall come: and I will fill this house with glory, saith the Lord of Hosts. The silver is mine, and the gold is mine, saith the Lord of Hosts. The glory of this latter house shall be greater than of the former, saith the Lord of Hosts: and in this place will I give peace, saith the Lord of Hosts."

In the four and twentieth day of the ninth month, in the second year of Darius, came the word of the Lord by Haggai the prophet, saying, "Thus saith the Lord of Hosts; Ask now the priests concerning the law, saying, If one bear holy flesh in the skirt of his garment, and with his skirt do touch bread, or pottage, or wine, or oil, or any meat, shall it be holy?" And the priests answered and said, "No." Then said Haggai, "If one that is unclean by a dead body touch any of these, shall it be unclean?" And the priests answered and said, "It shall be unclean."

Then answered Haggai, and said, "So is this people, and so is this nation before me, saith the Lord; and so is every work of their hands; and that which they offer there is unclean. And now, I pray you, consider from this day and upward, from before a stone was laid upon a stone in the temple of the Lord: since those days were, when one came to an heap of twenty measures, there were but ten: when one came to the pressfat for to draw out fifty vessels out of the press, there were but twenty. I smote you with blasting and with mildew and with hail in all the labours of your hands; yet ye turned not to me, saith the Lord. Consider now from this day and upward, from the four and twentieth day of the ninth month, even from the day that the foundation of the Lord's temple was laid, consider it. Is the seed yet in the barn? yea, as yet the vine, and the fig tree, and the pomegranate, and the olive tree, hath not brought forth: from this day will I bless you."

And again the word of the Lord came unto Haggai in the four and twentieth day of the month, saying, "Speak to Zerubbabel, governor of Judah, saying, I will shake the heavens and the earth; and I will overthrow the throne of kingdoms, and I will destroy the strength of the kingdoms of the heathen; and I will overthrow the chariots, and those that ride in them; and the horses and their riders shall come down, every one by the sword of his brother. In that day, saith the Lord of Hosts, will I take thee, O Zerubbabel, my servant, the son of Shealtiel, saith the Lord, and will make thee as a signet: for I have chosen thee, saith the Lord of Hosts."

ZECHARIAH

IN THE eighth month, in the second year of Darius, came the word of the Lord unto Zechariah the son of Berechiah, the son of Iddo the prophet, saying,

"The Lord hath been sore displeased with your fathers. Therefore say thou unto them, Thus saith the Lord of Hosts; Turn ye unto me, saith the Lord of Hosts, and I will turn unto you, saith the Lord of Hosts. Be ye not as your fathers, unto whom the former prophets have cried, saying, Thus saith the Lord of Hosts; Turn ye now from your evil ways, and from your evil doings: but they did not hear, nor hearken unto me, saith the Lord. Your fathers, where are they? and the prophets, do they live for ever? but my words and my statutes, which I commanded my servants the prophets, did they not take hold of your fathers? and they returned and said, Like as the Lord of Hosts thought to do unto us, according to our ways, and according to our doings, so hath he dealt with us."

Upon the four and twentieth day of the eleventh month, which is the month Sebat, in the second year of Darius, came the word of the Lord unto Zechariah the son of Berechiah, the son of Iddo the prophet, saying,

I saw by night, and behold a man riding upon a red horse, and he stood among the myrtle trees that were in the bottom; and behind him were there red horses, speckled, and white. Then said I, "O my lord, what are these?" And the Angel that talked with me said unto me, "I will shew thee what these be." And the man that stood among the myrtle trees answered and said, "These are they whom the Lord hath sent to walk to and fro through the earth."

And they answered the Angel of the Lord that stood among the myrtle trees, and said, "We have walked to and fro through the earth, and, behold, all the earth sitteth still, and is at rest." Then the Angel of the Lord answered and said, "O Lord of Hosts, how long wilt thou not have mercy on Jerusalem and on the cities of Judah, against which thou hast had indignation these threescore and ten years?" And the Lord answered the Angel that talked with me with good words and comfortable words.

So the Angel that communed with me said unto me, "Cry thou, saying, Thus saith the Lord of Hosts; I am jealous for Jerusalem and for Zion with a great jealousy. And I am very sore displeased with the heathen that are at ease: for I was but a little displeased, and they helped forward the affliction. Therefore thus saith the Lord; I am returned to Jerusalem with mercies: my house shall be built in it, saith the Lord of Hosts, and a line shall be stretched forth upon Jerusalem. Cry yet, saying, Thus saith the Lord of Hosts; My cities through prosperity shall yet be spread abroad; and the Lord shall yet comfort Zion, and shall yet choose Jerusalem."

Then lifted I up mine eyes, and saw, and behold four horns. And I said unto the Angel that talked with me, "What be these?" And he answered me, "These are the horns which have scattered Judah, Israel, and Jerusalem." And the Lord shewed me four carpenters. Then said I, "What come these to do?" And he spake, saying, "These are the horns which have scattered Judah, so that no man did lift up his head: but these are come to fray them, to cast out the horns of the Gentiles, which lifted up their horn over the land of Judah to scatter it."

I lifted up mine eyes again, and looked, and behold a man with a measuring line in his hand. Then said I, "Whither goest thou?" And he said unto me, "To measure Jerusalem, to see what is the breadth thereof, and what is the length thereof."

And, behold, the Angel that talked with me went forth, and another Angel went out to meet him, and said unto him, "Run, speak to this young man, saying, Jerusalem shall be inhabited as towns without walls for the multitude of men and cattle therein: for I, saith the Lord, will be unto her a wall of fire round about, and will be the glory in the midst of her.

"Ho, ho, come forth, and flee from the land of the north, saith the Lord: for I have spread you abroad as the four winds of the heaven, saith the Lord. Deliver thyself, O Zion, that dwellest with the daughter of Babylon. For thus saith the Lord of Hosts; After the glory hath he sent me unto the nations which spoiled you: for he that toucheth you toucheth the apple of his eye. For, behold, I will shake mine hand upon them, and they shall be a spoil to their servants: and ye shall know that the Lord of Hosts hath sent me.

"Sing and rejoice, O daughter of Zion: for, lo, I come, and I will dwell in the midst of thee, saith the Lord. And many nations shall be joined to the Lord in that day, and shall be my people: and I will dwell in the midst of thee, and thou shalt know that the Lord of Hosts hath sent me unto thee. And the Lord shall inherit Judah his portion in the holy land, and shall choose Jerusalem again. Be silent, O all flesh, before the Lord: for he is raised up out of his holy habitation."

And he shewed me Joshua the high priest standing before the Angel of the Lord, and Satan standing at his right hand to resist him.

And the Lord said unto Satan, "The Lord rebuke thee, O Satan; even the Lord that hath chosen Jerusalem rebuke thee: is not this a brand plucked out of the fire?" Now Joshua was clothed with filthy garments, and stood before the Angel. And he answered and spake unto those that stood before him, saying, "Take away the filthy garments from him." And unto him he said, "Behold, I have caused thine iniquity to pass from thee, and I will clothe thee with change of raiment." And I said, "Let them set a fair mitre upon his head." So they set a fair mitre upon his head, and clothed him with garments. And the Angel of the Lord stood by.

And the Angel of the Lord protested unto Joshua, saying, "Thus saith the Lord of Hosts; If thou wilt walk in my ways, and if thou wilt keep my charge, then thou shalt also judge my house, and shalt also keep my courts, and I will give thee places to walk among these that stand by. Hear now, O Joshua the high priest, thou, and thy fellows that sit before thee: for they are men wondered at: for, behold, I will bring forth my servant the Branch. For behold the stone that I have laid before Joshua; upon one stone shall be seven eyes: behold, I will engrave the graving thereof, saith the Lord of Hosts, and I will remove the iniquity of that land in one day. In that day, saith the Lord of Hosts, shall ye call every man his neighbour under the vine and under the fig tree."

And the Angel that talked with me came again, and waked me, as a man that is wakened out of his sleep, and said unto me, "What seest thou?" And I said, "I have looked, and behold a candlestick all of gold, with a bowl upon the top of it, and his seven lamps thereon, and seven pipes to the seven lamps, which are upon the top thereof: and two olive trees by it, one upon the right side of the bowl, and the other upon the left side thereof."

So I answered and spake to the Angel that talked with me, saying, "What are these, my lord?" Then the Angel that talked with me answered and said unto me, "Knowest thou not what these be?" And I said, "No, my lord." Then he answered and spake unto me, saying, "This is the word of the Lord unto Zerubbabel, saying, Not by might, nor by power, but by my spirit, saith the Lord of Hosts. Who art thou, O great mountain? before Zerubbabel thou shalt become a plain: and he shall bring forth the headstone thereof with shoutings, crying, Grace, grace unto it."

Moreover the word of the Lord came unto me, saying, "The hands of Zerubbabel have laid the foundation of this house; his hands shall also finish it; and thou shalt know that the Lord of Hosts hath sent me unto you. For who hath despised the day of small things? for they shall rejoice, and shall see the plummet in the hand of Zerubbabel with those seven; they are the eyes of the Lord, which run to and fro through the whole earth."

Then answered I, and said unto him, "What are these two olive trees upon the right side of the candlestick and upon the left side thereof?" And I answered again, and said unto him, "What be these two olive branches which through the two golden pipes empty the golden oil out of themselves?" And he answered me and said, "Knowest thou not what these be?" And I said, "No, my lord." Then said he, "These are the two Anointed Ones, that stand by the Lord of the whole earth."

Then I turned, and lifted up mine eyes, and looked, and behold a flying roll. And he said unto me, "What seest thou?" And I answered, "I see a flying roll; the length thereof is twenty cubits, and the breadth thereof ten cubits." Then said he unto me, "This is the curse that goeth forth over the face of the whole earth: for every one that stealeth shall be cut off as on this side according to it; and every one that sweareth shall be cut off as on that side according to it. I will bring it forth, saith the Lord of Hosts, and it shall enter into the house of the thief, and into the house of him that sweareth falsely by my name: and it shall remain in the midst of his house, and shall consume it with the timber thereof and the stones thereof."

Then the Angel that talked with me went forth, and said unto me, "Lift up now thine eyes, and see what is this that goeth forth." And I said, "What is it?" And he said, "This is an ephah that goeth forth." He said moreover, "This is their resemblance through all the earth." And, behold, there was lifted up a talent of lead: and this is a woman that sitteth in the midst of the ephah. And he said, "This is Wickedness." And he cast it into the midst of the ephah; and he cast the weight of lead upon the mouth thereof. Then lifted I up mine eyes, and looked, and, behold, there came out two women, and the wind was in their wings; for they had wings like the wings of a stork: and they lifted up the ephah between the earth and the heaven. Then said I to the Angel that talked with me, "Whither do these bear the ephah?" And he said unto me, "To build it an house in the land of Shinar: and it shall be established, and set there upon her own base."

And I turned, and lifted up mine eyes, and looked, and, behold, there came four chariots out from between two mountains; and the mountains were mountains of brass. In the first chariot were red horses; and in the second chariot black horses; and in the third chariot white horses; and in the fourth chariot grisled and bay horses. Then I answered and said unto the Angel that talked with me, "What are these, my lord?" And the Angel answered and said unto me, "These are the four spirits of the heavens, which go forth from standing before the Lord of all the earth. The black horses which are therein go forth into the north country; and the white go forth after them; and the grisled go forth toward the south country." And the bay went forth, and sought to go that they might walk to and fro through the earth: and he said, "Get you hence, walk to and fro through the earth." So they walked to and fro through the earth. Then cried he upon me, and spake unto me, saying, "Behold, these that go toward the north country have quieted my spirit in the north country."

And the word of the Lord came unto me, saying, "Take of them of the captivity, even of Heldai, of Tobijah, and of Jedaiah, which are come from Babylon, and come thou the same day, and go into the house of Josiah the son of Zephaniah; then take silver and gold, and make crowns, and set them upon the head of Joshua the son of Josedech, the high priest; and speak unto him, saying, Thus speaketh the Lord of Hosts, saying, Behold the man whose name is The Branch; and he shall grow up out of his place, and he shall build the temple of the Lord: even he shall build the temple of the

Lord; and he shall bear the glory, and shall sit and rule upon his throne; and he shall be a priest upon his throne: and the counsel of peace shall be between them both. And the crowns shall be to Helem, and to Tobijah, and to Jedaiah, and to Hen the son of Zephaniah, for a memorial in the temple of the Lord. And they that are far off shall come and build in the temple of the Lord, and ye shall know that the Lord of Hosts hath sent me unto you. And this shall come to pass, if ye will diligently obey the voice of the Lord your God."

And it came to pass in the fourth year of king Darius, that the word of the Lord came unto Zechariah in the fourth day of the ninth month, even in Chisleu; when they had sent unto the house of God Sherezer and Regemmelech, and their men, to pray before the Lord, and to speak unto the priests which were in the house of the Lord of Hosts, and to the prophets, saying, "Should I weep in the fifth month, separating myself, as I have done these so many years?" Then came the word of the Lord of Hosts unto me, saying, "Speak unto all the people of the land, and to the priests, saying, When ye fasted and mourned in the fifth and seventh month, even those seventy years, did ye at all fast unto me, even to me? And when ye did eat, and when ye did drink, did not ye eat for yourselves, and drink for yourselves? Should ye not hear the words which the Lord hath cried by the former prophets, when Jerusalem was inhabited and in prosperity, and the cities thereof round about her, when men inhabited the south and the plain?"

And the word of the Lord came unto Zechariah, saying, "Thus speaketh the Lord of Hosts, saying, Execute true judgment, and shew mercy and compassions every man to his brother: and oppress not the widow, nor the fatherless, the stranger, nor the poor; and let none of you imagine evil against his brother in your heart. But they refused to hearken, and pulled away the shoulder, and stopped their ears, that they should not hear. Yea, they made their hearts as an adamant stone, lest they should hear the law, and the words which the Lord of Hosts hath sent in his spirit by the former prophets: therefore came a great wrath from the Lord of Hosts. Therefore it is come to pass, that as he cried, and they would not hear; so they cried, and I would not hear, saith the Lord of Hosts: but I scattered them with a whirlwind among all the nations whom they knew not. Thus the land was desolate after them, that no man passed through nor returned: for they laid the pleasant land desolate."

Again the word of the Lord of Hosts came to me, saying,

"Thus saith the Lord of Hosts; I was jealous for Zion with great jealousy, and I was jealous for her with great fury. Thus saith the Lord; I am returned unto Zion, and will dwell in the midst of Jerusalem: and Jerusalem shall be called a city of truth; and the mountain of the Lord of Hosts the holy mountain. Thus saith the Lord of Hosts; There shall yet old men and old women dwell in the streets of Jerusalem, and every man with his staff in his hand for very age. And the streets of the city shall be full of boys and girls playing in the streets thereof.

"Thus saith the Lord of Hosts; If it be marvellous in the eyes of the remnant of this people in these days, should it also be marvellous in mine eyes, saith the Lord of Hosts? Thus saith the Lord of Hosts; Behold, I will save my people from the east country, and from the west country; and I will bring them, and they shall dwell in the midst of Jerusalem: and they shall be my people, and I will be their God, in truth and in righteousness.

"Thus saith the Lord of Hosts; Let your hands be strong, ye that hear in these days these words by the mouth of the prophets, which were in the day that the foundation of the house of the Lord of Hosts was laid, that the temple might be built. For before these days there was no hire for man, nor any hire for beast;

neither was there any peace to him that went out or came in because of the affliction: for I set all men every one against his neighbour. But now I will not be unto the residue of this people as in the former days, saith the Lord of Hosts. For the seed shall be prosperous; the vine shall give her fruit, and the ground shall give her increase, and the heavens shall give their dew; and I will cause the remnant of this people to possess all these things. And it shall come to pass, that as ye were a curse among the heathen, O house of Judah, and house of Israel; so will I save you, and ye shall be a blessing: fear not, but let your hands be strong. For thus saith the Lord of Hosts; As I thought to punish you, when your fathers provoked me to wrath, saith the Lord of Hosts, and I repented not: so again have I thought in these days to do well unto Jerusalem and to the house of Judah: fear ye not.

"These are the things that ye shall do; Speak ye every man the truth to his neighbour; execute the judgment of truth and peace in your gates: and let none of you imagine evil in your hearts against his neighbour; and love no false oath: for all these are things that I hate, saith the Lord."

And the word of the Lord of Hosts came unto me, saying,

"Thus saith the Lord of Hosts; The fast of

the fourth month, and the fast of the fifth, and the fast of the seventh, and the fast of the tenth, shall be to the house of Judah joy and gladness, and cheerful feasts; therefore love the truth and peace.

"Thus saith the Lord of Hosts; It shall yet come to pass, that there shall come people, and the inhabitants of many cities: and the inhabitants of one city shall go to another, saying, Let us go speedily to pray before the Lord, and to seek the Lord of Hosts: I will go also. Yea, many people and strong nations shall come to seek the Lord of Hosts in Jerusalem, and to pray before the Lord. Thus saith the Lord of Hosts; In those days it shall come to pass, that ten men shall take hold out of all languages of the nations, even shall take hold of the skirt of him that is a Jew, saying, We will go with you: for we have heard that God is with you."

The burden of the word of the Lord in the land of Hadrach, and Damascus shall be the rest thereof: when the eyes of man, as of all the tribes of Israel, shall be toward the Lord. And Hamath also shall border thereby; Tyrus, and Zidon, though it be very wise. And Tyrus did build herself a strong hold, and heaped up silver as the dust, and fine gold as the mire of the streets. Behold, the Lord will cast her out, and he will smite her power in the sea; and she shall be devoured with fire. Ashkelon shall see it, and fear; Gaza also shall see it, and be very sorrowful, and Ekron; for her expectation shall be ashamed; and the king shall perish from Gaza, and Ashkelon shall not be inhabited. And a bastard shall dwell in Ashdod, and I will cut off the pride of the Philistines. And I will take away his blood out of his mouth, and his abominations from between his teeth: but he that remaineth, even he, shall be for our God, and he shall be as a governor in Judah, and Ekron as a Jebusite. And I will encamp about mine house because of the army, because of him that passeth by, and because of him that returneth: and no oppressor shall pass through them any more: for now have I seen with mine eyes.

Rejoice greatly, O daughter of Zion; shout, O daughter of Jerusalem: behold, thy King cometh unto thee: he is just, and having salvation; lowly, and riding upon an ass, and upon a colt the foal of an ass. And I will cut off the chariot from Ephraim, and the horse from Jerusalem, and the battle bow shall be cut off: and he shall speak peace unto the heathen: and his dominion shall be from sea even to sea, and from the river even to the ends of the earth. As for thee also, by the blood of thy covenant I have sent forth thy prisoners out of the pit wherein is no water.

Turn you to the strong hold, ye prisoners of hope: even to day do I declare that I will render double unto thee; when I have bent Judah for me, filled the bow with Ephraim, and raised up thy sons, O Zion, against thy sons, O Greece, and made thee as the sword of a mighty man. And the Lord shall be seen over them, and his arrow shall go forth as the lightning: and the Lord God shall blow the trumpet, and shall go with whirlwinds of the south. The Lord of Hosts shall defend them; and they shall devour, and subdue with sling stones; and they shall drink, and make a noise as through wine; and they shall be filled like bowls, and as the corners of the altar. And the Lord their God shall save them in that day as the flock of his people: for they shall be as the stones of a crown, lifted up as an ensign upon his land. For how great is his goodness, and how great is his beauty! corn shall make the young men cheerful, and new wine the maids.

Ask ye of the Lord rain in the time of the latter rain; so the Lord shall make bright clouds, and give them showers of rain, to every one grass in the field. For the idols have spoken vanity, and the diviners have seen a lie, and have told false dreams; they comfort in vain: therefore they went their way as a flock, they were troubled, because there was no shepherd. Mine anger was kindled against the shepherds, and I punished the goats: for the Lord of Hosts hath visited his flock the house of Judah, and hath made them as his goodly horse in the battle. Out of him came forth the corner, out of him the nail, out of him the battle bow, out of him every oppressor together. And they shall be as mighty men, which tread down their enemies in the mire of the streets in the battle: and they shall fight, because the Lord is with them, and the riders on horses shall be confounded. And I will strengthen the house of Judah, and I will save the house of Joseph, and I will bring them again to place them; for I have mercy upon them: and they shall be as though I had not cast them off: for I am the Lord their God, and will hear them. And they of Ephraim shall be like a mighty man, and their heart shall rejoice as through wine: yea, their children shall see it, and be glad; their heart shall rejoice in the Lord.

I will hiss for them, and gather them; for I have redeemed them: and they shall increase as they have increased. And I will sow them among the people: and they shall remember me in far countries; and they shall live with their children, and turn again. I will bring them again also out of the land of Egypt, and gather them out of Assyria; and I will bring them into the land of Gilead and Lebanon; and place shall not be found for them. And he shall pass through the sea with affliction, and shall smite the waves in the sea, and all the deeps of the river shall dry up: and the pride of Assyria shall be brought down, and the sceptre of Egypt shall depart away. And I will strengthen them in the Lord; and they shall walk up and down in his name, saith the Lord.

Open thy doors, O Lebanon, that the fire may devour thy cedars. Howl, fir tree; for the cedar is fallen; because the mighty are spoiled: howl, O ye oaks of Bashan; for the forest of the vintage is come down. There is a voice of the howling of the shepherds; for their glory is spoiled: a voice of the roaring of young lions; for the pride of Jordan is spoiled.

Thus saith the Lord my God; Feed the flock of the slaughter; whose possessors slay them, and hold themselves not guilty: and they that sell them say, "Blessed be the Lord; for I am rich:" and their own shepherds pity them not. For I will no more pity the inhabitants of the land, saith the Lord: but, lo, I will deliver the men every one into his neighbour's hand, and into the hand of his king: and they shall smite the land, and out of their hand I will not deliver them. And I will feed the flock of slaughter, even you, O poor of the flock.

And I took unto me two staves; the one I called Beauty, and the other I called Bands; and I fed the flock. Three shepherds also I cut off in one month; and my soul loathed them, and their soul also abhorred me. Then said I, "I will not feed you: that that dieth, let it die; and that that is to be cut off, let it be cut off; and let the rest eat every one the flesh of another." And I took my staff, even Beauty, and cut it asunder, that I might break my covenant which I had made with all the people. And it was broken in that day: and so the poor of the flock that waited upon me knew that it was the word of the Lord.

And I said unto them, "If ye think good, give me my price; and if not, forbear." So they weighed for my price thirty pieces of silver. And the Lord said unto me, "Cast it unto the potter: a goodly price that I was prized at of them!" And I took the thirty pieces of silver, and cast them to the potter in the house of the Lord. Then I cut asunder mine other staff, even Bands, that I might break the brotherhood between Judah and Israel. And the Lord said unto me, "Take unto thee yet the instruments of a foolish shepherd. For, lo, I will raise up a shepherd in the land, which shall not visit those that be cut off, neither shall seek the young one, nor heal that that is broken, nor feed that that standeth still: but he shall eat the flesh of the fat, and tear their claws in pieces."

Woe to the idol shepherd that leaveth the flock! the sword shall be upon his arm, and upon his right eye: his arm shall be clean dried up, and his right eye shall be utterly darkened.

The burden of the word of the Lord for Israel, saith the Lord, which stretcheth forth the heavens, and layeth the foundation of the earth, and formeth the spirit of man within him. Behold, I will make Jerusalem a cup of trembling unto all the people round about, when they shall be in the siege both against Judah and against Jerusalem. And in that day will I make Jerusalem a burdensome stone for all people: all that burden themselves with it shall be cut in pieces, though all the people of the earth be gathered together against it. In that day, saith the Lord, I will smite every horse with astonishment, and his rider with madness: and I will open mine eyes upon the house of Judah, and will smite every horse of the people with blindness. And the governors of Judah shall say in their heart, "The inhabitants of Jerusalem shall be my strength in the Lord of Hosts their God."

In that day will I make the governors of Judah like an hearth of fire among the wood, and like a torch of fire in a sheaf; and they shall devour all the people round about, on the right hand and on the left: and Jerusalem shall be inhabited again in her own place, even in Jerusalem. The Lord also shall save the tents of Judah first, that the glory of the house of

David and the glory of the inhabitants of Jerusalem do not magnify themselves against Judah. In that day shall the Lord defend the inhabitants of Jerusalem; and he that is feeble among them at that day shall be as David; and the house of David shall be as God, as the Angel of the Lord before them. And it shall come to pass in that day, that I will seek to destroy all the nations that come against Jerusalem.

And I will pour upon the house of David, and upon the inhabitants of Jerusalem, the spirit of grace and of supplications: and they shall look upon me whom they have pierced, and they shall mourn for him, as one mourneth for his only son, and shall be in bitterness for him, as one that is in bitterness for his firstborn. In that day shall there be a great mourning in Jerusalem, as the mourning of Hadadrimmon in the valley of Megiddon. And the land shall mourn, every family apart: the family of the house of David apart, and their wives apart; the family of the house of Nathan apart, and their wives apart; the family of the house of Levi apart, and their wives apart; the family of Shimei apart, and their wives apart; all the families that remain, every family apart, and their wives apart.

In that day there shall be a fountain opened to the house of David and to the inhabitants of Jerusalem for sin and for uncleanness. And it shall come to pass in that day, saith the Lord of Hosts, that I will cut off the names of the idols out of the land, and they shall no more be remembered: and also I will cause the prophets and the unclean spirit to pass out of the land. And it shall come to pass, that when any shall yet prophesy, then his father and his mother that begat him shall say unto him, "Thou shalt not live; for thou speakest lies in the name of the Lord:" and his father and his mother that begat him shall thrust him through when he prophesieth. And it shall come to pass in that day, that the prophets shall be ashamed every one of his vision, when he hath prophesied; neither shall they wear a rough garment to deceive: but he shall say, "I am no prophet, I am an husbandman; for man taught me to keep cattle from my youth." And one shall say unto him, "What are these wounds in thine hands?" Then he shall answer, "Those with which I was wounded in the house of my friends."

Awake, O sword, against my shepherd, and against the man that is my fellow, saith the Lord of Hosts: smite the shepherd, and the sheep shall be scattered: and I will turn mine hand upon the little ones. And it shall come to pass, that in all the land, saith the Lord, two parts therein shall be cut off and die; but the third shall be left therein. And I will bring the third part through the fire, and will refine them as silver is refined, and will try them as gold is tried: they shall call on my name, and I will hear them: I will say, "It is my people:" and they shall say, "The Lord is my God."

Behold, the day of the Lord cometh, and thy spoil shall be divided in the midst of thee. For I will gather all nations against Jerusalem to battle; and the city shall be taken, and the houses rifled, and the women ravished; and half of the city shall go forth into captivity, and the residue of the people shall not be cut off from the city. Then shall the Lord go forth, and fight against those nations, as when he fought in the day of battle. And his feet shall stand in that day upon the mount of Olives, which is before Jerusalem on the east, and the mount of Olives shall cleave in the midst thereof toward the east and toward the west, and there shall be a very great valley; and half of the mountain shall remove toward the north, and half of it toward the south. And ye shall flee to the valley of the mountains; for the valley of the mountains shall reach unto Azal: yea, ye shall flee, like as ye fled from before the earthquake in the days of Uzziah king of Judah: and the Lord my God shall come, and all the saints with thee. And it shall come to pass in that day, that the light shall not be clear, nor dark: but it shall be one day which shall be known to the Lord, not day, nor night: but it shall come to pass, that at evening time it shall be light.

And it shall be in that day, that living waters shall go out from Jerusalem; half of them toward the former sea, and half of them toward the hinder sea: in summer and in winter shall it be. And the Lord shall be king over all the earth: in that day shall there be one Lord, and his name one. All the land shall be turned as a plain from Geba to Rimmon south of Jerusalem: and it shall be lifted up, and inhabited in her place, from Benjamin's gate unto the place of the first gate, unto the corner gate, and from the tower of Hananeel unto the king's winepresses. And men shall dwell in it, and there shall be no more utter destruction, but Jerusalem shall be safely inhabited.

And this shall be the plague wherewith the Lord will smite all the people that have fought against Jerusalem; their flesh shall consume away while they stand upon their feet, and their eyes shall consume away in their holes, and their tongue shall consume away in their mouth. And it shall come to pass in that day, that a great tumult from the Lord shall be among them; and they shall lay hold every one on the hand of his neighbour, and his hand shall rise up against the hand of his neighbour. And Judah also shall fight at Jerusalem; and the wealth of all the heathen round about shall be gathered together, gold, and silver, and apparel, in great abundance. And so shall be the plague of the horse, of the mule, of the camel, and of the ass, and of all the beasts that shall be in these tents, as this plague.

And it shall come to pass, that every one that is left of all the nations which came against Jerusalem shall even go up from year to year to worship the King, the Lord of Hosts, and to keep the feast of tabernacles. And it shall be, that whoso will not come up of all the families of the earth unto Jerusalem to worship the King, the Lord of Hosts, even upon them shall be no rain. And if the family of Egypt go not up, and come not, that have no rain; there shall be the plague, wherewith the Lord will smite the heathen that come not up to keep the feast of tabernacles. This shall be the punishment of Egypt, and the punishment of all nations that come not up to keep the feast of tabernacles.

In that day shall there be upon the bells of the horses, Holiness unto the Lord; and the pots in the Lord's house shall be like the bowls before the altar. Yea, every pot in Jerusalem and in Judah shall be holiness unto the Lord of Hosts: and all they that sacrifice shall come and take of them, and seethe therein: and in that day there shall be no more the Canaanite in the house of the Lord of Hosts.

MALACHI

THE burden of the word of the Lord to Israel by Malachi.

I have loved you, saith the Lord. Yet ye say, "Wherein hast thou loved us?" Was not Esau Jacob's brother? saith the Lord: yet I loved Jacob. And I hated Esau, and laid his mountains and his heritage waste for the dragons of the wilderness.

Whereas Edom saith, "We are impoverished, but we will return and build the desolate places;" thus saith the Lord of Hosts, They shall build, but I will throw down; and they shall call them The border of wickedness, and, The people against whom the Lord hath indignation for ever. And your eyes shall see, and ye shall say, "The Lord will be magnified from the border of Israel."

A son honoureth his father, and a servant his master: if then I be a father, where is mine honour? and if I be a master, where is my fear? saith the Lord of Hosts unto you, O priests, that despise my name. And ye say, "Wherein have we despised thy name?" Ye offer polluted bread upon mine altar; and ye say, "Wherein have we polluted thee?" In that ye say, "The table of the Lord is contemptible." And if ye offer the blind for sacrifice, is it not evil? and if ye offer the lame and sick, is it not evil? offer it now unto thy governor; will he be pleased with thee, or accept thy person? saith the Lord of Hosts. And now, I pray you, beseech God that he will be gracious unto us: this hath been by your means: will he regard your persons? saith the Lord of Hosts.

Who is there even among you that would shut the doors for nought? neither do ye kindle fire on mine altar for nought. I have no pleasure in you, saith the Lord of Hosts, neither will I accept an offering at your hand. For from the rising of the sun even unto the going down of the same my name shall be great among the Gentiles; and in every place incense shall be offered unto my name, and a pure offering: for my name shall be great among the heathen, saith the Lord of Hosts. But ye have profaned it, in that ye say, "The table of the Lord is polluted; and the fruit thereof, even his meat, is contemptible." Ye said also, "Behold, what a weariness is it!" and ye have snuffed at it, saith the Lord of Hosts; and ye brought that which was torn, and the lame, and the sick; thus ye brought an offering: should I accept this of your hand? saith the Lord. But cursed be the deceiver, which hath in his flock a male, and voweth, and sacrificeth unto the

Lord a corrupt thing: for I am a great King, saith the Lord of Hosts, and my name is dreadful among the heathen.

And now, O ye priests, this commandment is for you. If ye will not hear, and if ye will not lay it to heart, to give glory unto my name, saith the Lord of Hosts, I will even send a curse upon you, and I will curse your blessings: yea, I have cursed them already, because ye do not lay it to heart. Behold, I will corrupt your seed, and spread dung upon your faces, even the dung of your solemn feasts; and one shall take you away with it. And ye shall know that I have sent this commandment unto you, that my covenant might be with Levi, saith the Lord of Hosts. My covenant was with him of life and peace; and I gave them to him for the fear wherewith he feared me, and was afraid before my name. The law of truth was in his mouth, and iniquity was not found in his lips: he walked with me in peace and equity, and did turn many away from iniquity. For the priest's lips should keep knowledge, and they should seek the law at his mouth: for he is the messenger of the Lord of Hosts. But ye are departed out of the way; ye have caused many to stumble at the law; ye have corrupted the covenant of Levi, saith the Lord of Hosts. Therefore have I also made you contemptible and base before all the people, according as ye have not kept my ways, but have been partial in the law.

Have we not all one father? hath not one God created us? why do we deal treacherously every man against his brother, by profaning the covenant of our fathers? Judah hath dealt treacherously, and an abomination is committed in Israel and in Jerusalem; for Judah hath profaned the holiness of the Lord which he loved, and hath married the daughter of a strange god. The Lord will cut off the man that doeth this, the master and the scholar, out of the tabernacles of Jacob, and him that offereth an offering unto the Lord of Hosts.

And this have ye done again, covering the altar of the Lord with tears, with weeping, and with crying out, insomuch that he regardeth not the offering any more, or receiveth it with good will at your hand. Yet ye say, "Wherefore?" Because the Lord hath been witness between thee and the wife of thy youth, against whom thou hast dealt treacherously: yet is she thy companion, and the wife of thy covenant.

And did not he make one? Yet had he the residue of the spirit. And wherefore one? That he might seek a godly seed. Therefore take heed to your spirit, and let none deal treacherously against the wife of his youth. For the Lord, the God of Israel, saith that he hateth putting away: for one covereth violence with his garment, saith the Lord of Hosts: therefore take heed to your spirit, that ye deal not treacherously. Ye have wearied the Lord with your words. Yet ye say, "Wherein have we wearied him?" When ye say, "Every one that doeth evil is good in the sight of the Lord, and he delighteth in them;" or, "Where is the God of judgment?"

Behold, I will send my messenger, and he shall prepare the way before me: and the Lord, whom ye seek, shall suddenly come to his temple, even the messenger of the covenant, whom ye delight in: behold, he shall come, saith the Lord of Hosts. But who may abide the day of his coming? and who shall stand when he appeareth? for he is like a refiner's fire, and like fullers' soap: and he shall sit as a refiner and purifier of silver: and he shall purify the sons of Levi, and purge them as gold and silver, that they may offer unto the Lord an offering in righteousness.

Then shall the offering of Judah and Jerusalem be pleasant unto the Lord, as in the days of old, and as in former years. And I will come near to you to judgment; and I will be a swift witness against the sorcerers, and against the adulterers, and against false swearers, and against those that oppress the hireling in his wages, the widow, and the fatherless, and that turn aside the stranger from his right, and fear not me, saith the Lord of Hosts. For I am the Lord, I change not; therefore ye sons of Jacob are not consumed.

Even from the days of your fathers ye are gone away from mine ordinances, and have not kept them. Return unto me, and I will return unto you, saith the Lord of Hosts. But ye said, "Wherein shall we return?" Will a man rob God? Yet ye have robbed me. But ye say, "Wherein have we robbed thee?" In tithes and offerings. Ye are cursed with a curse: for ye have robbed me, even this whole nation. Bring ye all the tithes into the storehouse, that there may be meat in mine house, and prove me now herewith, saith the Lord of Hosts, if I will not open you the windows of heaven, and pour you out a blessing, that there shall not be room enough to receive it. And I will rebuke the devourer for your sakes, and he shall not destroy the fruits of your ground; neither shall your vine cast her fruit before the time in the field, saith the Lord of Hosts. And all nations shall call you blessed: for ye shall be a delightsome land, saith the Lord of Hosts.

Your words have been stout against me, saith the Lord. Yet ye say, "What have we spoken so much against thee?" Ye have said, "It is vain to serve God: and what profit is it that we have kept his ordinance, and that we have walked mournfully before the Lord of Hosts? And now we call the proud happy; yea, they that work wickedness are set up; yea, they that tempt God are even delivered." Then they that feared the Lord spake often one to another: and the Lord hearkened, and heard it, and a book of remembrance was written before him for them that feared the Lord, and that thought upon his name. And they shall be mine, saith the Lord of Hosts, in that day when I make up my jewels; and I will spare them, as a man spareth his own son that serveth him. Then shall ye return, and discern between the righteous and the wicked, between him that serveth God and him that serveth him not.

For, behold, the day cometh, that shall burn as an oven; and all the proud, yea, and all that do wickedly, shall be stubble: and the day that cometh shall burn them up, saith the Lord of Hosts, that it shall leave them neither root nor branch. But unto you that fear my name shall the Sun of righteousness arise with healing in his wings; and ye shall go forth, and grow up as calves of the stall. And ye shall tread down the wicked; for they shall be ashes under the soles of your feet in the day that I shall do this, saith the Lord of Hosts.

Remember ye the law of Moses my servant, which I commanded unto him in Horeb for all Israel, with the statutes and judgments.

Behold, I will send you Elijah the prophet before the coming of the great and dreadful day of the Lord: and he shall turn the heart of the fathers to the children, and the heart of the children to their fathers, lest I come and smite the earth with a curse.

END OF VOL. VI.

www.ingramcontent.com/pod-product-compliance
Lightning Source LLC
Chambersburg PA
CBHW021209230426
43667CB00006B/621